Salt & Light: Being the Hands and Feet of Christ
(in a cruel and dangerous world)

Salt & Light:
Being the Hands and Feet of Christ
(in a cruel and dangerous world)

CPT. M.D. Poole

Salt & Light: Being the Hands and Feet of Christ
(in a cruel and dangerous world)

D W B   P U B L I S H I N G
www.dwbpublishing.com

Salt & Light: Being the Hands and Feet of Christ
(in a cruel and dangerous world)

For Matson, Presley, and Reagan

"If your heart is wise, then my heart will be glad indeed." – Proverbs 23:15

Salt & Light: Being the Hands and Feet of Christ
(in a cruel and dangerous world)

Preface

'Can a cop be a Christian? Or inversely, can a Christian be a cop? These two questions call for not only an analysis of the "police subculture," one characterized by high rates of cynicism and both potential, anticipated, and experienced violence, but also an analysis of the perceptions and beliefs regarding the compatibility of Christianity and law enforcement'- Boston D. Ross.

When first writing this book, I contacted Ross, a police officer himself, as he had conducted a survey in spring of 2016 to answer those questions through a combination of surveys and theological research. His preliminary research was compiled using the answers to numerous surveys of three specific societal subsets to include civilians, law enforcement officers, and clergy.

From this research came a type of *"theology for law enforcement,"* a theology which presented a Biblical and spiritual basis upon which a law enforcement officer could justify actions or aspects of the profession which are, at times, deemed incompatible with Christian tenets.

Ross and I saw that his research and my personal experience validated each other. It was also found, through our own exhausted means, that the need for further research on the subject is great, and the findings of such research could be beneficial to not only current law enforcement officers, but also civilians seeking potential employment, the civilian population at large, and the clergy who may minister to police officers.

In Matthew 5:13-16 Jesus tells us that we are the *"salt of the earth"* and *"light of the world."* Saying of the salt *"But if the salt loses its saltiness, how can it be made salty again? It is no longer good for anything, except to be thrown out and trampled underfoot"* and of the light *"A town built on a hill cannot be hidden. Neither do people light a lamp and put it under a bowl. Instead they put it on its stand, and it gives light to everyone in the house. In the same way, let your light shine before others, that they may see your good deeds and glorify your Father in heaven."* Jesus was calling those who serve the Lord and challenging them to not lose their spiritual fervor but to share their beliefs through Christ-like actions that would give glory to His Father.

It is no secret that attempting to deal with the emotional strain of our positions as police officers, can lead to unsettling issues that are at times, overwhelming. Sometimes in our effort to become resilient to these evils, we place faith in impractical solutions and lose sight of our convictions. This is no more less a truth for a Christian officer attempting to navigate the sometimes, torturous nature of his or her chosen career field. Throughout this writing I try to bring to light the challenges officers' face, especially those who hold Christian beliefs, and the grace I found that led me to overcome my personal spiritual battles, enabling me to have a stronger walk with God.

In this writing I hope that pulling the curtain back and displaying one life behind the badge can add to this theology, with biblical knowledge and personal testimony, a view of the raw nature of law enforcement and the feelings one may exhibit while

still in the course of their duties, while still present-
ing literature which adheres to the standards of
Christian principals.

I don't purport to be a theologian of any sort and
apologize in advance for any number of lengthy sen-
tences found throughout, as I have become accustomed to that style of writing within the many years
of my law enforcement career. Take note that I also
feel scripture is best shown within context and not
on its own. To take one verse out of a chapter and
not show it surrounded within the respective scriptural content only denigrates the experience of
God's word.

All scripture quoted is of the NIV or ESV, unless
otherwise stated.

Acknowledgement

I would first and foremost say that writing this book was no easy task. I find it very difficult to speak about my life, some of my experiences, and regretfully, it is best that some things were left unsaid. I cannot thank God enough for placing a friend like my wife, Mendy, into my life. Mendy was unaware of the gathering storm that she would fight living the life of a LEO'S wife and although she would not accept the following truth, she shows me a love I feel I could never repay.

I am also grateful for my brother, Officer Andrew Poole, who played a huge role in my law enforcement career, whether he knew or not. Having him beside me at some of my darkest moments, although hidden, helped push me to maintain my character as an officer and display, as a leader, a mantra of selflessness that I now see at work in him.

Furthermore, extending my warm thanks to Officer Boston D. Ross is essential. Ross's investigative need to answer questions about law enforcement and Christianity, led me to question the way I viewed my service. When first observing Ross's questions in his 2016 survey, *Law Enforcement Officers and Christianity: Toward a Joint Theology for Law Enforcement*, I thought to myself, of course you can be a Christian and an officer. Examining that very possibility helped me to see that I was failing my Lord and Savior by not fully implementing the gifts He had blessed me with, while in the performance of my duties. Ross was a welcomed voice throughout this process, and I pray that God continues to work through him to further His Kingdom.

Finally, with all my heart, I wish to thank Kristi and Richard Neace, founders of Badge of Hope Ministries. Kristi and Rick work together along with various other first responder groups, to have a greater impact for Christ. Kristi's words, throughout her numerous publications, helped my wife to see a different side of life in law enforcement, and helped me, to combat my callousness toward her. Kristi and Rick dedicated their personal time to review this work and offer their cordial insight. I pray that their works will be blessed, that their lives will be blessed, and that their ministry thrives in bringing others to Christ.

Introduction

In 1996 a young boy walked into his 7th grade classroom, 13, unenthused, unimpressed and unaware that by the end of class, he'd be changed. The teacher was out for the day and a lackadaisical substitute had taken charge of the class advising there would be "free time" for the students to do as they wished, so long as their activity was done quietly.

The boy set to work quickly writing a letter to his father, a member of the Armed Services, currently stationed overseas in Saudi Arabia. This wasn't the first time the boy's father had been stationed away from him, but he recalled it being the hardest leave he had dealt with, and as pen met paper, so did tears. No pause transpired before the dam broke and tears fell uncontrollably down his face. An even shorter amount of time occurred before the once laidback teacher of children lost his patience and decided to teach a lesson in class after all.

Despite the Man's persistent demands for the youth to stop crying, as this was a disturbance to the classroom, the boy simply could not and found bottling his emotions near impossible. The substitute, obviously being well-educated and versed in child psychology, decided the best course of action to end such a disruption, and return order to the outlandish chaos plaguing his classroom, was corporal punishment.

One could only imagine the thoughts others had while classmates watched the boy being led to a chalkboard in the room. The boy, on the other hand, only felt sad and alone. All the noise and steady mumbling coming from the class and teacher alike, fell away until he heard one word, "reach."

The man advised the boy to reach as high as he could touch on the chalkboard and, having done so, drew a line with chalk directly above it. He advised the boy to touch the line that had been drawn, keeping his fingers on the line until told otherwise, which just so happened to be the end of class.

Up until this point in life the boy hadn't always been the best at listening, but even at such a young age, he knew what it meant to respect authority, even if unjustly given. He had been taught not to stir up events or fight, being told, or at least he believed, that affrays and disruptions could lead to his father being disciplined and possibly losing rank. There were many times unbeknownst to his father, that he had been pushed, hit and pulled toward unwanted physical encounters, only to hide his emotions inward and do the only thing he knew he could do for his father, turn the other cheek.

This time was different though. This time the boy realized that what he had been doing wasn't only for his father's service, instead, it was service itself. This was the one way, right then and there, the boy could honor his father. A new feeling took hold of him, and with tears streaming, leaving a trail on his young, unsullied face, he reached as high as he could and touched the line as commanded, unashamed and unafraid. He fought through the pain as he stretched, and thinking of his father as he hurt, his heart swelled with pride.

That wasn't the day the boy decided to be a police officer, but it was the day the seed for service was planted. He realized that day that love is sacrifice and came to believe that selfless service was

15

giving whatever he could, in whatever way he could, whenever he could. The boy's definition and concept of service changed over the years and strengthened into the realization that faith through works is, indeed, love in action—indeed a selfless love lived. Unfortunately, he also ended that day believing that pain, sometimes being a part of that sacrifice, was something that he had to bear alone, an idea that nearly cost him his life twenty-two years later.

~ * ~

I am that boy. I am a law enforcement veteran, husband, father, confessed sinner, practicing Christian, and a recovering alcoholic. My ambition for this book is not to tell you the story of my life but a hope that reading these chapters will give you the tools, through scripture, to be a true servant, whether a believer in Christ or not. As a peace officer, I know that dark trails, characterized by the worst of human nature and depravity are more prevalent on our walk through this life. Often seeing the evils of this world daily, officers bear more than just the pains of their own afflictions, usually leading to coping mechanisms which are detrimental not only to our physical and spiritual selves but to others as well.

Time and again we realize that while trying to be strong, we've done so by leaning on our own understanding of this system. And in doing so, we create a prison for ourselves which some officers never escape, except through dreadful means that are catastrophic to our loved ones, blue family or not. It is through my faith in Christ Jesus that I believe even if caged we can see beyond the bars. As the Apostle Paul displayed by his letters while incarcerated and in kind, you can hold this statement as truth. A man without faith is a man without hope.

Captain Matt Poole

Salt & Light: Being the Hands and Feet of Christ
(in a cruel and dangerous world)

~ One ~

"So you also, when you have done everything you were told to do, should say, 'We are unworthy servants; we have only done our duty.'" ~Luke 17:10

I have always been a man of few words. As a child, my father often said that I didn't talk a lot but when I did, there was importance or a need. Looking back, I find that assessment to be somewhat true. To be honest, I'm sure I levied my fair share of insults, mounted verbal attacks against many, and let others bear witness to a whole new dimension of foul language that would never be described as warranted, let alone important. I was, on the other hand, blessed with the gift of getting my point across in as few words necessary to gain the attention and compliance of others, if of course, words were even needed. This gift was only verbal in nature, and I found expressing my feelings in any input other than lyrics or poems, difficult. For these reasons I never believed I would be writing a book, or at least a non-fiction one. As for police work, articulation of the law came easy, unlike the articulation of my emotions, the meanings of which, were typically hidden in long thought out phrasings of words that only I could understand, and others could only imagine.

When I first started writing this book, the thought of expressing so much about my personal life never occurred to me, experiences in law enforcement maybe, but not myself in general. My intent was to stay as far away from a memoir as possible and to convey, through biblical scripture, a reminder of what it is to be a good servant, more importantly, a godly servant. I found it hard to separate my personal life from professional, as I will detail later, and can only pray that the message is not lost throughout the following pages.

I began my law enforcement career in 2003, graduating from the police academy at twenty years of age, somewhat naïve, yet ready to work. I became a commissioned officer in January 2004, and soon took my first full-time paid job as a real-life peace officer February 3rd of the same year. I wore a hand-me-down vest from my grandfather, service weapon on loan from my brother, and a fresh pair of Danners that would not be replaced for another eight years. The vehicle I was assigned had a bench seat with a faulty lock, rotators on top that froze, and could hardly top 85mph going uphill. One officer on shift, backup thirty, or more, minutes out, nine dollars an hour, and yet, I loved every minute of it. I counted myself blessed, and still do, that I was brought up and mentored in my tenure by seasoned and knowledgeable officers.

I considered myself to be a "good" officer. I didn't protest my lot, took whatever assignment I was given or whatever change in shift hours came my way, without showing distress. I asked for no compliment, wanted no applause, never stayed idle, performed as delegated, fielded my calls for service quickly, eyes on work and opinion to myself unless requested, and lodged no complaint. I believed service was selfless, not something you laud over anyone, an action, or set of actions, which you never remind the public that you perform and, definitely not something you did for recognition. I always believed that if you had to remind people of all the good things you had done, then you probably messed up a lot. As far as I was concerned, the department and I had an agreement—I work what I'm scheduled, and you pay me every two weeks. No one owed me a thing, and to this day, my approach remains the same.

As a young officer I was callous, although not completely heartless. It's almost scary now seeing how easy it was to become near emotionless while dealing with people who were in the middle of the worst day of their lives on most occasions. As cops are known to say, "People typically don't call us to tell us they had a great day or to celebrate their birthday with them."

It wasn't that I didn't care; I was just doing my job as a *"good"* officer. I came to realize what made callousness so easy for me, and what was probably one of my biggest downfalls, was being trained not to use religion, in general, or a belief in God, as a tool while working. This is not to say that nobody ever said faith wasn't a big part of how they did the job, but it was highly frowned upon to bring the word of God into *"battle,"* while in the middle of a domestic disturbance, trying to restrain a resisting drunk, working a teen suicide, or fighting for your life.

The idea behind this anti-religious inclination was that steadfast religious ideals could conflict with experiences encountered and tolerated while in the discharge of duties. Yes, small prayers and quick quips were often muttered while topping 130mph in a Crown Vic that should have been decommissioned 100,000 miles prior to the *"hot"* call we received. But, as it was, most calls and most cases ended with the same dark humor and foul language most of us were used to and I fear, most of us needed to help cope with the visual and physical trauma we endured almost daily. The warrior mindset had been birthed, the patrolman had taken the wheel, and I took a back seat.

Almost fifteen years later, I am not that same young officer. I know that I've made, *even if through small motions*, positive impacts in people's lives. The atmosphere has changed though. I have changed. And by some beautiful and tragic moments, my understanding of true service has changed, which leads me to believe I've also left negative impacts in the wake of a career and lifestyle that are everlasting. As I said, the warrior mindset had taken control and the patrolman was on autopilot. A lot of emphasis was not placed on the guardian mindset early in my career and if it was, that insight was overlooked. The warrior mindset, taught as though it was paramount to physical and emotional survival, took precedence over that of the guardian. All the same, the model made sense to me and still does, it just doesn't take precedence anymore.

When times were bad, the old saying rang true, *'sometimes there's justice, sometimes there's just us,'* a slogan which made perfect sense when you believed that the community owed you nothing, nor did they want to give you anything. That even if the public did, they weren't supposed to and, even if they could, you couldn't take it or in most cases, wouldn't. No gratuities, no thanks, and if there was any local support, it was all but invisible. There was nothing personal about the experience, it was just business as usual. The eyes opened, the vest went on, the Vic started up and I served the public, justly and fairly, without want.

Working in a small town or even your standard police beat, for a long period of time, changes you—changes the way you work and how you see people, even the individuals with whom you had contact on what seemed like a daily basis. You memorize the streets, houses and people in your beat, to the point you can see one small thing out of order. You learn and become a part of people's lives. A very intimate relationship matures. You build rapport that helps clear calls quickly, and if done correctly over the years, the officer could become such a staple in their lives that most people could be talked into handcuffs.

I've always prided myself on that concept and still practice using communication as a restraining tool, so long as it is safe to do so, and although I am far from afraid of using force, I try to welcome it as a last resort. As a plus, communicating also keeps me from having to chase most suspects, as the rabbit in me died a long time ago, probably even before my relic of a Crown Vic. Unfortunately, over time, the effectiveness with which I served all but died as well.

I found the very definition of my service to be a half-truth. Even though my morality was straight-edge, following that compass while performing duties and the various tasks assigned to me was hard, usually leading just left of true north. When the uniform went on a whole other person took control. Dealing with constant domestic abuse, sexual assaults, crimes against children, deaths and other tragedies left me emotionless. I was a man in a uniform, just and fair, no more, no less. I later realized that I willfully caused a separation at the core of my

23

Christian beliefs, effectively letting me serve as a human and not as Christ.

The Bible shows us that true service requires true love. Paul writes in 1 Corinthians 13 1-3, *"If I speak in the tongues of men or of angels, but do not have love, I am only a resounding gong or a clanging cymbal. If I have the gift of prophecy and can fathom all mysteries and all knowledge, and if I have a faith that can move mountains, but do not have love, I am nothing. If I give all I possess to the poor and give over my body to hardship that I may boast, but do not have love, I gain nothing."*

All of us learn of our humanity at some point, but when do we learn the mortality of our actions? Paul is stating that all movements we, as humans could make, whether in good nature or not, hold no weight in time without love. Paul goes on to offer us a narration of what love does in verses 4-8, understanding that he is not defining a feeling, but an action.

"Love is patient, love is kind. It does not envy, it does not boast, it is not proud. It does not dishonor others, it is not self-seeking, it is not easily angered, it keeps no record of wrongs. Love does not delight in evil but rejoices with the truth. It always protects, always trusts, always hopes, always perseveres. Love never fails." Paul then continues in vv. 8-13 to show the fragility of human action and reinforce loves enduring promise— *"But where there are prophecies, they will cease; where there are tongues, they will be stilled; where there is knowledge, it will pass away. For we know in part and we prophesy in part, but when completeness comes, what is in part disappears. When I was a child, I talked like a child, I thought like a child, I*

reasoned like a child. When I became a man, I put the ways of childhood behind me. For now we see only a reflection as in a mirror; then we shall see face to face. Now I know in part; then I shall know fully, even as I am fully known. And now these three remain: faith, hope and love. But the greatest of these is love."

Love is perfect and eternal. We as humans are not. There is no end to the influences or vices, no limit to the schemes or illusions that we will write off as just, fair or Godly in our own minds that keep us from willfully practicing and showing the love of God through our actions, some of which are division, desire, despair and fear. Police officers deal with these four destructive evils on a daily basis and are equally involved in a number of events that present paradoxical concerns between their religious morality and the actions they may have to take within the performance of their duties. This includes being a sinner who is called to place their humanity at the service of society, swearing to serve and protect all citizens in their jurisdiction, showing grace and mercy while governing, and the taking of a human life or other uses of force.

Salt & Light: Being the Hands and Feet of Christ
(in a cruel and dangerous world)

~ Two ~

"Do your best to present yourself to God as one approved, a worker who does not need to be ashamed, and who correctly handles the word of truth." - 2 Timothy 2:15

Regretfully, the use of force is necessary, and often leads to long-lasting effects of trauma to the officer and offender alike. When you've had to fight for your life, or been injured in the line of duty, your senses change. You begin to view the general public in a different way. Your mind stays constantly alert, leading to hypervigilance, and in turn, you begin to isolate yourself from other people. This separation helps us, in effect, to remove ourselves from the feelings needed to show compassion or understanding and allows us to focus on self-preservation and accomplishing the mission when difficulties present themselves. This also presents a burden to those attempting to operate within a potentially violent job field while affirming their faith, as some people consider the very nature of force to be sinful, whether called upon or not.

The use of force police officers use is determined by the various acts of violence, or potentially violent circumstances, they may encounter on numerous occasions. There is a sense of legitimacy in the force police officers use, as the guidelines for said use is strictly enforced by various departments and courts alike. Although the use of force may be justified, violent actions can still present inconsistencies that stir cause for an internal debate within the Christian police officer. This may happen more times than not as officers are faced with instances of violence on an almost daily basis.

Exodus 20:13 states *"you shall not murder."* Numerous other verses throughout the Bible warn us against the bloodshed of others. Furthermore, we are also presented with verses such as Psalm 82:4 that states, *"Rescue the weak and needy; Deliver them out of the hand of the wicked."* A reminder of our obligation to protect those who may be in danger.

Officers encounter offenders killing other humans. They work death and homicide scenes and are sometimes called into circumstances that may require them to use deadly force, whether it be in their defense or the defense of another. There is evil in the world that sometimes requires a deadly action be taken to stop it. As police officers, our moral obligation is to stop evil from harming or killing those within our care. Although we practice using fewer physical means to bring about an end to any use of force, we also understand when no nonviolent methodologies can be employed to effectively end violence, force escalation becomes our obligation.

While I can't give you a definitive answer to justify or condemn the use of force, I can offer that we can change others propensity to use such force against us by imitating the love of Christ in service to others, and help transform the perspective of our actions in the communities we serve.

One of the nine principles of policing, attributed to Sir Robert Peel, is that police always maintain a relationship with the public that gives reality to the historic tradition that the police are the public and the public are the police. Peel stated the police act only as members of the public who are paid to give full-time attention to duties which are incumbent on every citizen in the interests of community welfare and existence. There are many different ideas and models when attempting to defining community policing. A simple overview of community policing focuses on building ties and working closely with members of the communities.

Bertus Ferreira's writing, *The Use and Effectiveness of Community Policing in a Democracy* (1996), would add, *'Community policing is a philosophy of full service personalized policing, where the same officer patrols and works in the same area on a permanent basis, from a decentralized place, working in a proactive partnership with citizens to identify and solve problems.'*

Although the construction of community policing is largely attributed to the civil rights movement during the 1960's and 70's, the movement accelerated in 1982 with the national magazine, *The Atlantic Monthly*'s publication of an article entitled *Broken Windows*, and federal funds made available through the Office of Community Oriented Policing Services (COPS), fueled the implementation and development throughout the 1990's helping to cultivate programs and studies such as the *Fair & Impartial Policing Perspective*, a science-based approach that focuses on unconscious biases that effected officers perceptions of citizens. This wasn't to affirm some belief that bias were formed due to racism in policing but tried to address the police culture and the cynicism often found in it.

Cynicism, according to Niederhoffer (1967), requires a person to draw certain conclusions about circumstances. This would suggest an inherent thought process is developed due to negative encounters with repeated offenders and situations, not only a byproduct of the paramilitary structure of most departments, but also the warrior mindset we are accustomed to.

I believe that we, as officers, must look at our-selves objectively in this matter, then we should in effect, help to ensure citizens take an objective look at their own perception of officers, as their culture also produces its own cynicism. Average people are constantly subjected to misinformation about peace officers. Media and Hollywood alike have been con-sistent in their portrayal of the police. The police are made out to be ignorant, uneducated, and vil-lainous, on almost every platform whether it is a children's cartoon or blockbuster drama. Even if an officer is glorified, generally they're portrayed as the anti-hero, an out of bounds lawman hell bent on revenge or darkly immoral in their pursuit of justice. Sadly, not much help is offered by the government to change the perspective of citizens, leaving the burden at the officer level within their local de-partments.

I remember I was asked once what I thought the biggest issue was with society's perceptions of law enforcement. I said society's issue was not being able, or willing, to deal with its own problems. There is no being neighborly anymore or civil with each other. Even good people lack the ability to be civil with each other over the smallest issues. People just can't simply walk next door and speak to some-one about small issues like noise, trash, parking too close; you know, small, little, mostly non-criminal issues, and generally they can't do that because other people can't be bothered to listen. Civility is just too much of an inconvenience. So, what do they do? They call the police, because that's what you're supposed to do now, right?

The police, who, among the other tasks they have, such as drug enforcement, property crimes prevention, criminal investigations, also have to take these calls for service. Some calls for service turn into criminal investigations, but most calls, as I'm sure any officer would agree, turn out to be nothing but civil matters. They turn out being calls from people who can't, or won't, be civil with each other, and in the end, call the police to handle the matter. In turn, the officer must contact another party that the complainant is calling about, and of course they're never happy to see the police. Although they may be generally polite while dealing with them, the grudge is held against the officer or department, for simply answering a call for service as required of them.

A perfect example of this, although small in nature, is the use of fireworks. We all know every officers favorite game of "gun shots or fireworks." The calls are nonstop and overwhelming in most cases. Now some of those calls need to be dealt with, but most of the contacts the officers make are with good people, popping small fireworks with their children. We try to be polite and give warnings because who doesn't want them to have fun or who doesn't remember doing the same thing when they were young? It's when you keep getting called back to the same place that a citation is eventually issued or the negative encounter occurs. I hate having to tell a father that he can't pop fireworks with his kids, we turn into the bad guys, the *fun* police, the "you should be out finding real criminals" people; and we should, but we can't. We get called, we respond, and in turn people's perception of law enforcement has turned bad.

Granted, there are bad apples out there, and trust me, they don't stay officers long because we police ourselves. In the same way, we should educate our public. Citizens need to realize that until they can learn to get along over the smallest of things, police are going to receive calls for service, and they are going to respond to those calls because that's what the City and its citizens want and pay them to do.

Police want to help and get great joy out of helping people with problems. Sometimes we are needed to mediate and generally both sides are happy with the outcome. What officer doesn't love a good contact? When the police are belittled, mocked or purely shown hatred because they answer a call for service, it causes a bad perception for both police and the general public. The common perception that police are contacting you simply because they want to ruin your good time or have a power trip is simply inaccurate.

Most people could never understand what life is like, not have a set schedule or never be off duty. They don't understand the lack of time we get to experience with families or opportunities missed out on. They don't comprehend what it's like to be faced with evil, to carry the burdens of fighting it, and to have your every move, decision and word challenged, mocked, picked apart or criticized. I don't think you will find any other profession painted as poorly with a broad brush, while dealing with the same issues, other than those in Christian Ministry.

An example of pastoral obligation in the Bible is

found in 1 Peter 5:2-3. *"Shepherd the flock of God that is among you, exercising oversight, not under compulsion, but willingly, as God would have you; not for shameful gain, but eagerly; not domineering over those in your charge, but being examples to the flock."*

Pastors are required to shepherd their flocks, provide counsel and support to church members during challenging times, receive confessions of sin and provide direction on repentance. Pastors follow biblical principles in order to be examples to church members and adhere to a biblically set standard of moral virtues including strength of character, grace, love, caring, and humility. Pastors often teach others by reflecting on their own mistakes and are held to a higher standard of behavior to effectively guide others.

A servant is a servant with or without a gun and badge. Clergy and officers both find themselves duty bound and expected to perform task adequately and appropriately. They are both compelled to act whenever called upon. For example, a priest may be called to intercede on behalf of a parishioner, while an officer is called upon, and must intercede, to stop the commission of a crime. Regrettably, academies don't offer hours on how to incorporate our Christian beliefs while working in an immoral world, or to address the issues of exercising our faith while in uniform.

Most of the training I received throughout my career consisted of copious amounts of literature, audio clips and video presentations covering the subjects of Racial Profiling, Cultural Diversity and Community Policing. Almost all the information focused on the division of race at the human level, none of the material ever touched on the personal division of spirit. Many teachers suggested that you had to "have faith" in order to make it throughout your career, but no one ever elaborated on a way to maintain it. In the end, we were still left with a choice between the warrior and guardian mentalities. Which is best in the police community? That opinion, of course, is divided.

In early 2011, I couldn't shake this feeling of true disconnect between the country and the police. People have been fighting with the police since first implemented, but it felt as if the pressure was building, and it was only a matter of time before the powder keg blew. I reevaluated my impressions of the guardian and warrior mindsets and started trying to teach officers to lean more on the guardian mentality, to show people through our acts as constitutional police officers, that we cared about each one of their liberties, whether agreed upon or not.

A guardian is generally described as a defender, protector or keeper, a person who looks after, and is legally responsible for someone who is unable to manage their own affairs. A warrior is typically described as a brave or experienced soldier or fighter, whose actions will revolve around them in order to be effective and persistent, while adapting to challenges and adversity.

In my opinion, I felt one couldn't operate as an effective police officer by solely relying on one of the two mindsets, as this job, and the very definition of the code of ethics, shows us we need to utilize both mindsets to accomplish that task. I tried to show officers that maintaining the guardian mindset as the primary course of action, was of more benefit to their careers, and to the community. I'd often say, "You have to walk into every call, or up to every stop as a guardian, with the ability to become a warrior in a nanosecond." I said this also knowing and advising, that of course, there are exceptions to this way of thinking, as this job is fluid in nature, and learning to flip that switch and maintain control was an ability that needed to be mastered and done so quickly.

The biggest hang-up, I found, was that most young officers had a perceived notion that if they were to give up their warrior mentality, they would end up being hurt, killed or have the same happen to another officer, due to their actions. What they didn't realize was that they didn't have to give up anything. Just because an officer walks as a guardian, doesn't mean he or she is not a warrior. If anything, it means they are one and the same, only placing others before self, as a servant.

I was very vocal in telling officers to commit in everything they did. I asked them to commit to their words, their actions, decisions, arrests, force, community, and family. I even coined the phrase "commit it or quit it," which I jokingly used often, as a fix all solution to most problems they encountered on duty. I had a hope that officers would see, that, in their committing to the code of ethics and truly practicing community policing as a guardian, they were not just putting themselves and the Department in good standing with the community, they were growing a supporting community that would fight for them.

I envisioned if all officers could take that stance, then perhaps we could make a loud enough voice in opposition to the divide. A voice that was willing to watch and protect our backs. I felt that the Police

Nation was going to need that support more than ever, but I failed to address the spiritual dissent of the country within my thoughts and words.

Then it exploded August 9, 2014, in Ferguson Missouri.

As if the "hands up, don't shoot" narrative wasn't a good enough catalyst for division, the death of Eric Garner in July 2014 only contributed to the wave of violence that was to come against the police. On December 20, 2014, Ismaaiyl Abdullah Brinsley murdered Rafael Ramos and Wenjian Liu, two on-duty New York City Police Department officers, as they sat in their patrol unit near the intersection of Myrtle and Tompkins Avenue. The wall went up immediately. The country was starting to come apart as sides were being taken, and it became abundantly clear, that it was time for the warrior.

I remember making multiple pleas openly, and in private, asking Officers to remember that as a majority, people truly did care about them and what happened to them. Of course, no one likes being pulled over or having to deal with the police, it's a very embarrassing situation in most cases, but the fact remained that respect was given on a large account. I expressed my opinion that the loudest voice was never that of the majority, asking that they not take what the minority was doing out on the majority they served. I started seeing, and hoped officers did too, that people in general were becoming very upset with the steady stream of violence against police officers and sympathetic to the pains we felt as brothers, during a time of loss and tragedy. Sadly, this wasn't the first tragedy to befall the Blue Nation during that time, and it wouldn't be the last.

On August 28, 2015, Deputy Darren H. Goforth, a

ten-year veteran of the Harris County Sheriff's Office, was gunned down in cold blood while filling his car with gas. I'm hard-pressed to describe the horror we truly felt. Goforth's murder not only shook officers to their core, but a nation of civilians woke up and decided to say, "enough is enough." The support shared by everyone was something I had never witnessed in my career up to that point. I didn't know what to think, and sometimes, didn't know how to act. I was confused and caught off guard by the change I saw occur.

People were constantly coming up just to say "thank you" or tell us they were sorry about the loss of one of our brothers. The prodigious support was just something I didn't know how to address. It's sad to reflect and say I felt weird being thanked for doing my job, especially by total strangers. I trained two officers during that time and had to stop going out to eat because people wouldn't let us pay for our own meals. I did slowly become accustomed to display of empathy and used the newly found support as a means to continue teaching the idea that community policing, truly does make a difference. Yet, with our growing visual support, the division in America continued to increase drawing a line across the nation.

On July 7, 2016, at 7:04 in the morning, I posted the following to Facebook, '*To say things are going to get ugly is an understatement. Things have been ugly for some time now and are only getting worse. For those in the fight, stay safe, come home, and know that the majority of the communities you serve care about and respect you.*'

I had a horrifying feeling I couldn't shake and didn't know why. Later, the desperate echoes of my wife's voice brought my fears to fruition. At 8:58 that evening, the deadliest event in U.S. law enforcement since the September 11th attacks, occurred in Dallas Texas, killing five officers and injuring nine others. That day marked the first time, as an officer, I cried in front of a civilian. My wife had a new experience all her own at home. My children were not sheltered from the realities of my job and knew exactly what their mother's demeanor and frantic search for information online meant. Those realities hit home as my wife scrolled on a picture of DART Officer Brent Thompson, the first DART officer to be killed in the line of duty since the department's inception, and a familiar face to my son.

Organizations willing to compromise a moral principal as fundamental as the divinity of life, and begin soliciting the inherent unlawfulness of visual hate, openly assassinating public servants, only perpetuated more conflict and did little to stir the "guardian." When the brutal systematic murder of police officers, for no other reason than their chosen profession, begins to be lauded and viewed as anything other than evil and unacceptable, the ability to foster any different type of relationship with society, other than that of the reactive warrior and lawless civilian, seems almost unrealistic, if not totally impossible.

Some believe the most important thing we can do as citizens is tell our government when it's wrong, but as Christian citizens, our primary concern is showing others how to do what is right. Between the civil unrest, false narratives, misinformation and downright outlandish excuses used to propagate violence; the country seemed to be less interested in solidarity and more interested in coming together to pick sides. Peace officers found themselves thrown in the middle, attempting to settle the discourse and discourage further violence, although the graft, and sometimes corruptive nature of some city governments, led to all-out chaos and the singling out of the police force to be painted as the architects attempting to divide the nation itself. With little vocal support from our nation's leaders, the capital found its whipping boy.

Something had to change, and nothing seemed to be working. Police organizations were trying to address personal differences in the communities, most times focusing only on the aftereffects of acts fueled by division, spurring anger and driving the spade further into the ground.

Police officers have always been held to a higher standard, and sometimes been disgusted by those very words, especially when spoken by someone who wouldn't wear them. It isn't abstract to believe that people, believing in a higher standard, would hold themselves to that standard as well. As a nation, we need to be given an example of Christ-like love, and who better to teach that example than the public servant?

Police generally consider themselves to have a systematic view of all human knowledge, viewing the common officer as a *"Jack of all trades."* We often state that in our line of work we wear multiple hats. The officer, the guidance counselor, the therapist, the consoler, the list could go on. As officers, we have been gifted with a special opportunity to present the standard of Christ on a world stage, every day we go to work, every call we respond to, every life we touch.

The thought of changing a world view, or even the world, by means of love is probably seen as naïve by most, especially officers. The point remains, in my opinion, that we, as Christians, have become spiritually lazy in our efforts to not only display our faith but to bring that faith to others, simply because we've accepted that what is written has been written and there is no need for further intervention on anyone else's behalf. This fault is caused not only by our view of the Bible but also because of our view of God in most circumstances. I viewed Scripture as concrete, but in a negative way. It was as if the end had already been written and I knew who would win. My thoughts were, if all this was coming to pass, then what good was I doing trying to change a world that would no doubt turn on God, bringing about tribulation? The chalk line on civilization's fall had already been struck and there was no need to deviate from it. In other words, if there could never be peace on earth through our own measures, then why bother at all? I soon realized how flawed a view this was.

Who was I to limit God? God does not love us out of necessity, He loves us for our sake, and He wants us to love each other in that very way. To what end would He require this of us? To the very end. Who are we to say when this system will end? Because it is written in words breathed into life by God? Yes, take these words as truth because they are, but don't for a minute believe that we can limit God to His own words, that we have Him trapped in a corner, that He cannot do the impossible. God wants us to love each day as though there were no end, with a hope that all His sons and daughters would know

His peace.

I am by no means attempting to distribute some new doctrine or develop a theology separate from God's word. I am just stressing the fact that when we begin to limit God to His words, we in turn undermine His omnipotence and make Him a figure that operates within man's reality and time.

The moment we stop viewing Scripture as dead words spoken in the past, or referencing a story that has already been told, and realize that Scripture is alive and has been since first inspired, is nothing short of a personal epiphany. It's a sudden and striking realization that the story hasn't ended, although parts have been told, but you are ever such a part of that same story as those that were spoken of long ago. Right now, we are in what will be the story of furthering God's Kingdom. What part will you play?

Salt & Light: Being the Hands and Feet of Christ
(in a cruel and dangerous world)

~ Three ~

"You, my brothers and sisters, were called to be free. But do not use your freedom to indulge the flesh; rather, serve one another humbly in love." - Galatians 5:13

Division has, and will always be, an obstacle. Division exists between the police and the community, the people that support us and those that don't, and within the police organization itself. As strong as the bond among the brotherhood may be, partitions still thrive throughout the thin blue line. Even though there is a tight knit brotherhood, its beliefs, morals and standards by which it's held together, turn on the tide of the very sea of blue, which made it evident.

Romans 12:3-8 speaks of humble service in the body of Christ. *"For by the grace given me I say to every one of you: Do not think of yourself more highly than you ought, but rather think of yourself with sober judgment, in accordance with the faith God has distributed to each of you. For just as each of us has one body with many members, and these members do not all have the same function, so in Christ we, though many, form one body, and each member belongs to all the others. We have different gifts, according to the grace given to each of us. If your gift is prophesying, then prophesy in accordance with your faith; if it is serving, then serve; if it is teaching, then teach; if it is to encourage, then give encouragement; if it is giving, then give generously; if it is to lead, do it diligently; if it is to show mercy, do it cheerfully."* 9-13 follows up on love in action, *"Love must be sincere. Hate what is evil; cling to what is good. Be devoted to one another in love. Honor one another above yourselves. Never be lacking in zeal, but keep your spiritual fervor, serving the Lord. Be joyful in hope, patient in affliction, faithful in prayer. Share with the Lord's people who are in need. Practice hospitality."*

In his letters, Paul called on the Christian community to come together and use the different gifts given to them to strengthen the church and the community, and to share the message of God's grace and love. As servants, we can look to this passage as a pathway to fixing division. If we view the body referenced as the community we serve or as the collective nation, then we can view the police as being a member of that body with the gift of service.

In our roles as peace officers we find ourselves in the very position to do all these things; prophesy, (if not by speech then with our actions), serve, teach, encourage, give generously, lead and show mercy. To do this though, an officer must be able to depart from a skeptical state of mind and put love into action. I believe that exercising our gift of service is an act of love, and in such aspects of affection, our service must be sincere.

Of course, it only makes sense that a police officer avoids evil and clings to "what is good," devoting themselves to one another, and honoring one another above themselves. The act of keeping spiritual fervor, being joyful in hope and patient in our afflictions, is not some alien concept. In fact, it's a perfect representation of the stoic way we move forward, mourning loved ones, facing new challenges, and still serving with hope. Officers must be constantly mindful of what being a servant really means and show our brothers in blue and our community family, that our oath has not been forgotten.

Numbers 30:2 states, *"If a man vows a vow to the Lord, or swears an oath to bind himself by a pledge, he shall not break his word. He shall do according to all that proceeds out of his mouth,"* and Deuteronomy 23:21-23, *"If you make a vow to the Lord your God, you shall not delay fulfilling it, for the Lord your God will surely require it of you, and you will be guilty of sin. But if you refrain from vowing, you will not be guilty of sin. You shall be careful to do what has passed your lips, for you have voluntarily vowed to the Lord your God what you have promised with your mouth."*

Peace officers affirm to an oath called the Code of Ethics. An oath that if truly believed and fulfilled, should make an impact, not only in the lives of those touched throughout their careers, but in their lives as well. It is through those actions promised, that the community they serve will have nothing to fault them with. The Code reads as follows:

Peace Officer Code of Ethics

AS A LAW ENFORCEMENT OFFICER, my fundamental duty is to serve the community; to safeguard lives and property; to protect the innocent against deception, the weak against oppression or intimidation, and the peaceful against violence or disorder; and to respect the constitutional rights of all persons to liberty, equality and justice.

I WILL keep my private life unsullied as an example to all and will conduct myself in a manner that does not bring discredit to me or to my agency. I will maintain courageous calm in the face of danger, scorn or ridicule; develop self-restraint; and be constantly mindful of the welfare of others. Honest in thought and deed in both my personal and official life, I will be exemplary in obeying the laws of the land and the regulations of my department. Whatever I see or hear of a confidential nature or that is confided to me in my official capacity will be kept ever secret unless revelation is necessary in the performance of my duty.

I WILL never act officiously or permit personal feelings, prejudices, political beliefs, aspirations, animosities or friendships to influence my decisions. With no compromise for crime and with relentless prosecution of criminals, I will enforce the law courteously and appropriately without fear or favor, malice or ill will, never employing unnecessary force or violence and never accepting gratuities.

I RECOGNIZE the badge of my office as a symbol of public faith and I accept it as a public trust to be held so long as I am true to the ethics of the police service. I will never engage in acts of corruption or bribery, nor will I condone such acts by other police officers. I will cooperate with all legally authorized agencies and their representatives in the pursuit of justice.

I KNOW that I alone am responsible for my own standard of professional performance and will take every reasonable opportunity to enhance and improve my level of knowledge and competence.

I WILL constantly strive to achieve these objectives and ideals, dedicating myself before God to my chosen profession... LAW ENFORCEMENT.

~ * ~

The other standard of service for recognizing our fundamental duties as Christian police officers is found in the word of God. In fact, I think it's safe to state that every paragraph of the Code of Ethics can be corroborated in the book of Proverbs alone.

A well-known fact in our line of work is that reaching out with help doesn't always go the way we plan, but I'm still a believer in putting actions over words. As Christian officers we need to help teach people to exercise faith over apathy. It's not just someone else's job, it's ours.

Proverbs 21:13 it states, *"He who shuts his ear to the cry of the poor will also cry himself and not be answered"* and in 22:2, *"the rich and the poor meet together; the Lord is the Maker of them all."*

Philippians 2:4 reminds us, *"do not merely look out for your own personal interests, but also for the interests of others,"* and in 1 John 3:17-18 it says, *"But whoever has the world's goods, and sees his brother in need and closes his heart against him, how does the love of God abide in him? Little children, let us not love with word or with tongue, but in deed and truth."*

As officers, we are often called to heartbreaking situations, where we find that others really could have helped someone, but instead, they passed judgment, and to our disappointment, we find some of our brethren manifesting the same contempt. Some of the ignorance habitually displayed, can be downright hateful in nature. I remember once, a picture was posted of a man, known by most as a local, who was sleeping in the City park. Of course, in true Facebook fashion, a long rant with absolutely no outward thought followed it. A thread of comments about the man possibly being a "rapist" or "drug user" accompanied the photo, and as one could assume, so did calls for service, as some were angry that a homeless person was in fact, homeless. Many loving and caring people came together to build a wonderful park, showing not only that they cared about the community but the people in it. Now, in that same community, others were tearing down a person they did not know, didn't care to know, and couldn't be bothered to help. Since when was it more Christian to take a picture and write a post with drawn conclusions than to be human? I knew the man and talked to him almost every day I worked. I tried my best to ensure he had water, food, and a place to stay. Although, often he didn't want any help, he never turned down an opportunity for me to just make sure he was doing alright.

In Proverbs 31: 8-9 we are called upon by God to give stability to the land by means of justice, warning that heavy exactions will bring it to ruin. We are told to speak up for those who cannot speak for themselves, and not only judge fairly those who are destitute, but to defend the rights of the poor and needy.

Mark 10:45 tells us that Jesus himself came to be a servant *"For even the Son of Man did not come to be served, but to serve, and to give his life as a ransom for many."*

When officers finally view the problem in the nation as a spiritual one, we can understand it will take physical examples of love to begin healing. Spiritual warfare requires spiritual warriors, which means the bar is set higher for those of Christian faith and even higher for those in a supervisory role.

In the effort to solidify my convictions and bring my public service closer to Christ like service, I began searching scripture vigorously, eagerly devoted to changing the way I, and others, viewed that service and allowing me to bring God into my work. I was on fire and found a kindred spirit in the Apostle Paul. His letters to the various churches inspired me, and I viewed them as such great guides for service. I thought if Paul, through all his faults could become a new man and great servant of God, nothing could keep me from achieving that goal as well, nothing that is, except myself.

My problem was my human understanding of love. I thought I was doing a better job of being a servant of Christ, and in ways I was, but I was keeping myself from reaching a full understanding of love, because I couldn't correctly define it.

On Sunday July 22nd, 2018, I woke and started getting dressed for work. I prayed as I always did while putting my vest and uniform on, asking that God help me to do work that would glorify Him, thanking Him for the gifts of my family, and praying for guidance. I had been putting together writings for some time, hoping to share a message with officers, to encourage a new definition of service that might take wave throughout the ranks of blue. Before going to church, I prayed again, asking God that He would let me know the message, that is, if He wanted me to spread one in the first place.

That Sunday, certain members and visitors of the church had just come back from a weeklong camp focused on service, and catering to the mentally and physically impaired, and as a man got up to tell his story, I got my answer. The man stated that he had been charged with the full care of a man that suffered from shaken baby syndrome. He came to a point in his story where they had gone to the pool with everyone, and although the man couldn't swim, he simply rocked him back and forth in the water.

He didn't think much of it until he remembered words in Matthew 25, *"For I was hungry and you gave me something to eat, I was thirsty and you gave me something to drink, I was a stranger and you invited me in, I needed clothes and you clothed me, I was sick and you looked after me, I was in prison and you came to visit me. Then the righteous will answer him, 'Lord, when did we see you hungry and feed you, or thirsty and give you something to drink? When did we see you a stranger and invite you in or needing clothes and clothe you? When did we see you sick or in prison and go to visit you? The King will reply, 'Truly I tell you, whatever you did for one of the least of these brothers and sisters of mine, you did for me."* Tears fell from the man's eyes when he said he looked down to see he was swinging Jesus back and forth in the water.

I realized that I, even though I had been focused on serving like Jesus, had still been failing to continuously see the Jesus in front of me. I started seeing the divisiveness in me that was still present. I knew it was time to stop leaning on my own understanding and open my eyes to not only see Christ in the people I loved, but to see an opportunity to serve everyone as Christ without preconception.

I could hear Martin Luther say, *"I beg you, blow your nose a bit, to make your head lighter and the brain clearer."* And Jesus to the doubting, *"How long must I be with you? How long must I put up with you?"* (Matthew 17:17)

They say you never stop learning until the day you die. Lesson learned day 12,971.

~ Four ~

*"We few, we happy few, we band of brothers—
for whoever sheds his blood with me today shall be
my brother." - William Shakespeare*

I often wondered if I should even pen this chapter. The thought bounced back and forth within my mind for quite some time. Not knowing how the words would be taken, or if they would be taken at all, weighed heavy on my heart, but I felt it wise to recall the changing atmosphere within the brotherhood itself as it contributes to what I would call, a thinning blue line.

Though I could put together example upon example to lead you along a storyline of separation among officers of all callings and creed, I find it best to address this issue briefly, if I can without being laconic, as I fear my words may be taken out of context or even denigrate the message I believe God is calling me to pass on.

On September 27th, 2010, I put on my uniform as any other day, but this day I took extra care to present myself as best I could. My boots were shined once again, every hair in place and finely shaved. It was the day we would be laying a brother to rest. Cpl. David Ralph Slaton, 56, had been killed in the line of duty when he struck a cow in the roadway near the Oklahoma border. The resulting impact pushed his vehicle into oncoming lanes of traffic, where he was hit by a southbound semi. Many would tell you that David was nothing more than a large teddy bear of a man in a tan Trooper uniform, kind and gentle. To this, I can attest and affirm.

The emotions ran deep upon arrival to the service. Hundreds of uniformed police officers and countless civilians congregated with nothing left but standing room to pay their respects. Every officer spoke to each other, giving their sympathies. There were hugs exchanged and tears shed. This was the thin blue line as big and bold as ever, swimming together in a room full of brown Stetsons, chocolate wranglers, and blue polyester.

The ride to the interment was no less spectacular. Had it not been for the judge riding in the vehicle with me, I would have completely lost it when I turned the corner and saw child after child, hands over their hearts, pictures of thanks being held high, and flags waving. I remember telling my wife that it was the most awe-inspiring and amazing display that I never wanted to see again.

Fast-forward March 5, 2016. I sat in a large stadium watching brothers and sisters in blue and tan line up in support of Officer David Hofer. I rode in a procession in his honor and piled in along others to be a part of his service. Many things got to me. His last call, the drums and pipes, his fiancé speaking, and his father. I stood there in his honor, not shaken, until I started to see his memorial wreaths fall. The men attending them started lying them down. Every time I saw one laid down, it hit me harder than the one before. But the real hurt came after his father spoke. He made a request that all officers break protocol and turn to embrace one another. To my left, I was met with a gracious hug, to my right, nothing but contempt.

I was reminded again of the derision that continues to float throughout the blue sea. Some might have attributed it to the events of the year, sixteen officers killed thus far if I recall correctly. Some may have credited it to the emotional state that most officers had been in for some time due to the violence toward officers across the nation, or even qualified it as being emotionally numb in the moment. No, I tell you, it was disgust. This man wearing a uniform and shield just like me carried nothing but disdain about his face. He was a separate entity from the surrounding flock, a black sheep. This was far from any sad case of badge fatigue or blue falconry, it was the absolute will to stand as an island among men, dispersed from any theory of a physical or emotional brotherhood. I fear, in the end, we only have ourselves to blame for the condescension that continues to cling to our shields.

Some officer may blame the academies, the new generations or any number of ridiculously mundane courses implemented mandatorily on the force. Others might blame the age of the officer, be it true age or years of service. Whether we want to accept it or not, truth lies in the fact that this is a cultural issue systemic to law enforcement. Outside stimulus planted seeds within our hardened ground, a union of blue and blood, but there was just enough dirt on that foundation and just enough enrichment from vitriolic members to fuel the influence of division in a milieu known for solace, protection, and like-mindedness.

We are a strong family, of this I am certain, and I love each of my brothers and sisters. I would and will support them all to the end of their endeavors, but that does not mean I will cast blind eyes on the faults that live in our own house. The old refrain mentioned earlier, "sometimes there's justice;

sometimes there's just us," has long faded to the whisper, "sometimes there's those we trust." I deeply love my blue family and the love that flows throughout a community of bluebloods is nothing short of remarkable, but I find that even though we are in a world that continues to scrutinize every waking action and every settling decision, we tend to be the most critical of ourselves in a long line of antagonists. Maybe we should focus less on 'putting people in their places' and focus more on putting ourselves in the place that directs them to where they need to be.

~ Five ~

"Whoever serves me must follow me; and where I am, my servant also will be. My Father will honor the one who serves me." - John 12:26

As discussed briefly the police organization is not immune from division, but I believe that the division officers face at a personal level is a paramount discussion that should be evaluated, before tackling the impediments of bringing a nation of blue bloods together.

The normal daily routines and duties of a police officer allow them to experience situations and encounters that are generally seen as not being congruent with the morality, spirituality or belief structures held by most people, civilian or sworn. Constant exposure to vicious felonies, savage animalistic acts, grief and suffering weigh on the mind, soul and body. As a result, we tend to isolate ourselves causing a division that separates us further from empathizing with others and in turn keeps us from effectively serving them. This characteristic in the police culture only exacerbates difficulties the Christian police officer must face in their work and service of God.

Jesus stated, *"Every kingdom divided against itself will be ruined, and every city or household divided against itself will not stand."* (Matthew 12:25).

You don't have to be a practicing Christian to understand this truth. However, if we are to take the Lord's words as truth and put them into practice, we must understand that if the kingdom, city and household divided will come to ruin, so will the divided individual. For this very reason, we must break the societal norms of policing that enable us to withstand the pressures we endure and reeducate ourselves to appropriately care for our own wellbeing, as we fight the good fight.

Let me make this very clear, pretending something doesn't affect you is still just pretending. Most police officers get really good at living two lives, or at least they think they do. I know I did. We try to separate work from home, home from work, and it's understandable. You just had that fight with your significant other before beginning your tour of duty; of course, you're going to leave that at home. You worked a fatal 10-50 (wreck) before going 42 (ending tour of duty), yeah, you're going to want to leave some details out when you are around family.

We try to clear our heads of the issues that cause us distress, and get our minds set on work, not only for our safety but the safety of our brothers. What we need to remember is although separating home from work is necessary at times, it is also vital as Christians that we do not separate the very essence of ourselves and beliefs at either place.

Holding the Code of Ethics presented earlier as the example, the same attributes that would define an officer in excellent standing, should also define us at home. We should strive to be the same person in both places. As Christians we need to understand the lifestyle that God calls us to live coincides with the moral lifestyle we are challenged to accept as peace officers. It is possible to be the same person at both places, in both positions, and it is much easier to manage one life than two. Mastering solidarity can be difficult though, as anything can be, and requires discipline, faith and patience.

In chapter 16 of Proverbs it says, *"To humans belong the plans of the heart, but from the Lord comes the proper answer of the tongue. All a person's ways seem pure to them, but motives are weighed by the Lord. Commit to the Lord whatever you do, and he will establish your plans. The Lord works out everything to its proper end— even the wicked for a day of disaster"* and *"In their hearts humans plan their course, but the Lord establishes their steps."*

If we commit ourselves to the example of Christ and lean on God's word, we alleviate the doubts caused by things we can't see, explain or understand, thus freeing us for righteous service, whether that be the Husband as the Christian head of the family, or God's calling of us in service of others.

Doubts are often caused by things we can't describe or explain that occur not only in our lives but the lives of others we are invited in as servants. It is imperative that we not only focus on our physical wellbeing but our spiritual health as well.

Jesus said, *"Love the Lord your God with all your heart and with all your soul and with all your mind and with all your strength;"* advising that this was the most important commandment. In 1 Samuel 12:24 we are told, *"But be sure to fear the Lord and serve him faithfully with all your heart; consider what great things he has done for you."*

We work as peace officers to build up and strengthen our physical resilience to the daily abuse and evil we deal with. We pour everything we have into making an impenetrable exterior, focusing on the physical aspects of being a servant that we neglect our spiritual resistance, only in disservice to ourselves. Love is the key here, as true service is love and true love is sacrifice, both examples set by Christ and God.

Matthew 12: 33-37 states, *"Either make the tree good and its fruit good, or else make the tree bad and its fruit bad; for a tree is known by its fruit. Brood of vipers! How can you, being evil, speak good things? For out of the abundance of the heart the mouth speaks. A good man out of the good treasure of his heart brings forth good things, and an evil man out of the evil treasure brings forth evil things. But I say to you that for every idle word men may speak, they will give account of it in the Day of Judgment. For by your words you will be justified, and by your words you will be condemned."*

If by our very words we are to be justified and condemned, how much more will we be judged by our actions? People's actions are their hearts in motion, something we as Christians can reflect on personally.

In Romans 12: 9, Paul describes love in action saying *"Love must be sincere. Hate what is evil; cling to what is good."* Proverbs 9:10 says, *"The fear of the Lord is the beginning of wisdom, and knowledge of the Holy One is understanding."*

This *"wisdom"* that leads to eternal life, hinges on the understanding that God is love.

Philippians 2 calls us to be like-minded with Jesus, having the same love, being one in spirit and of one mind, adding that we do nothing out of selfish ambition or vain conceit. We are also given, within the same chapter, an explanation of the very nature of Christ being an example to service in 5-8, *"In your relationships with one another, have the same mindset as Christ Jesus: Who, being in very nature God, did not consider equality with God something to be used to his own advantage; rather, he made himself nothing by taking the very nature of a servant, being made in human likeness. And being found in appearance as a man, he humbled himself by becoming obedient to death—even death on a cross."*

In His example, Christ wanted to show us the nature of the love He calls us to have through service and God showed us the nature of his love through the gift of His Son. Although we may find ourselves limited in our own definition of God's love through words, we are never limited in the ways we can show that love in service. 1 John 4 reminds us that God is love, and of the sacrifice He made because of His love for us, stating, *"Whoever does not love does not know God, because God is love. This is how God showed his love among us: He sent his one and only Son into the world that we might live through him. This is love: not that we loved God, but that he loved us and sent his Son as an atoning sacrifice for our sins."*

Focus for a moment on the life of service Jesus led, being humble and putting others above himself (*although in a position of authority*), with no conceit or self-ambition, obedient to the point of death. Isn't this already a life that most of us as peace officers purport living?

1 John 3:16 states *"This is how we know what love is: Jesus Christ laid down his life for us. And we ought to lay down our lives for our brothers and sisters."*

Christ is calling us to lie down far more than our physical lives in terms of blood and breathe in service to others. In laying down our lives we lay down every aspect of it. The time we spend building up earthly wealth and treasures, all things that will pass away, chasing after the wind. If we retrain our minds to serve as Jesus did, we should never have any moment wasted or toiled over as if a burden. Do we desire to gain earthly wealth and defend dogmatic principals of human institutions, or do we desire to have a relationship with God as our heavenly Father and Creator?

Throughout Ecclesiastes the author supports a narrative that everything is meaningless. *"There is no remembrance of the men of old, and even those who are yet to come will not be remembered by those who follow"* (v. 1:11).

The teacher states that wisdom, pleasure, toil, advancement, and riches are meaningless, and in example, shows how none of them will stand the test of time.

"For with much wisdom comes much sorrow; the more knowledge, the more grief" (v. 1:18), and, *"I denied myself nothing my eyes desired; I refused my heart no pleasure. My heart took delight in all my labor, and this was the reward for all my toil. Yet when I surveyed all that my hands had done and what I had toiled to achieve, everything was meaningless, a chasing after the wind; nothing was gained under the sun"* (v. 2:10-11). He continues, *"So my heart began to despair over all my toilsome labor under the sun. For a person may labor with wisdom, knowledge and skill, and then they must leave all they own to another who has not toiled for it. This too is meaningless and a great misfortune,"* (v. 2:20-21). *"Whoever loves money never has enough; whoever loves wealth is never satisfied with their income. This too is meaningless,"* (v.5:10). And, *"For who knows what is good for a person in life, during the few and meaningless days*

60

they pass through like a shadow? Who can tell them what will happen under the sun after they are gone?" (v. 6:12). In conclusion, the Teacher offers, *"Now all has been heard; here is the conclusion of the matter: Fear God and keep his commandments, for this is the duty of all mankind. For God will bring every deed into judgment, including every hidden thing, whether it is good or evil"* (vv. 12:13-14). This reminds us again as Proverbs 22:2 shadows, that The Lord is the maker of us all, and in the end one thing is certain, we will all be judged.

Every human thing we do passes away. To know God and show Him reverent fear is to love like God. Every act of ours on Earth will be forgotten, except for our acts of love, because love is never ending. Serving as Christ, we break the bonds of futility summarized in Ecclesiastes and set an example that will not be elapsed, as love does not answer to time. If we accept this as truth, it frees us to be joyfully obedient and delivers us from earthly limits. Focusing on God's Kingdom around us, ensures that wisdom gained is of purpose, our work is not in vain and unprofitable, our riches are gifts of the spirit, our pleasure is in Christ, and our love everlasting. In this way we put to death our earthly convictions and cast off the pointless veneer of this world to become alive in Jesus and find ourselves blessed beyond all measure. No work of love is meaningless, when the glory is given to God.

If we, as Christians, are choosing to hold the apostles and Christ as an example of servitude, but failing to exercise our faith in the same manner and with the same fervor as our brothers in Christ and the Lord Himself did while under true persecution, then our lack of dedication is reprehensible, and our silence disrespectful to their sacrifices made.

Should we find ourselves more apt to defend an earthly institution, leading other believers to do things inconsistent with our duties to God and serving the personal interest of ourselves or Man, then we are nothing more than careerist. As Christian police officers we should be determined to perform our duties as disciples so that our actions reflect Gods message and our works are seen as labors of love lasting in perpetuity.

The reflections of Proverbs 24:1-12 guide us to gain knowledge of God through wisdom and understanding, staying distant from the ways of the wicked. Saying 25 (Proverbs 24:10-12) reminds us that not only are we responsible for our own strength (*faith*) but it is our duty to rescue follow brothers in Christ who are living lives that lead to death. We, in fact, find ourselves morally bound through the following words, *"If you falter in a time of trouble, how small is your strength! Rescue those being led away to death; hold back those staggering toward slaughter. If you say, "But we knew nothing about this," does not he who weighs the heart perceive it? Does not he who guards your life know it? Will he not repay everyone according to what they have done?"* We also gain from this passage, an understanding of our calling to protect life, both physical and spiritual.

~ Six ~

"Let us not become weary in doing good, for at the proper time we will reap a harvest if we do not give up." ~ Galatians 6:9

I don't know that I could ever accurately term a word that could describe the combination of emotions officers must stomach. Amongst the gambit of those endured, I'm inclined to believe that helplessness is the most devastating to the spirit. In the midst of complete chaos, police officers find themselves calm and collected because they have been trained to not fixate on emotion but to focus on the task at hand and bring about resolution to disorder. Our very lives, and the lives of others, depend on us viewing turmoil as information, taking in that information, and committing to actions that will change the situation.

This is of little consolation to the peace officer who finds themselves helpless. In almost everything we do, we find purpose. Even if we are just a small a part of what is occurring, we experience joy in closure. It's when there is absolutely nothing we can do to change an outcome that we are at our weakest as officers. Not having the power to help is a horrible feeling that can take the most seasoned officer on a rollercoaster ride of emotions. It's a hard lesson learning you can be vulnerable. It's a harder one learning how to accept it.

I recall working a fatal accident early one year that involved three young teenage girls. I worked many scenes before that where unnaturally horrific and have seen some horrid sights that touched me in ways I'll never be able to explain but this completely unnerved me.

I was called by dispatch and sent to the major 10-50 just outside of city limits. I had to walk up a slight embankment to access the site where the ATV the girls were riding had been pushed by another vehicle when it was struck on the highway below. I'll never forget topping that hill and hearing those painful screams. All three of the juveniles were pinned in the ATV. One was unconscious and believed to be low-sick, one deceased and the other, her sister, was severely injured.

I went to work quickly assessing the situation, but a dreadful reality became clear, there would be absolutely nothing I could do. I couldn't get them out, I couldn't treat them, and I couldn't bring the weeping girl's sibling back to life.

We had a full boat of EMS, fire personnel and law enforcement on scene running up and down the hill, engine to engine, trying to relay information or get lifesaving tools from the bottom to the top. This was one of the rare times, in all my years of service, that I felt completely helpless, or more accurately, useless. There are very few things that leave as haunting a feeling than watching the innocence slip from a child's eyes. Sadly, death and injury, from crashes and other similar incidents, are not the only way officers witness that loss.

There's a different kind of sickening feeling you get working offenses involving physical or sexual abuse, domestic, or not. As hard as you try, it is near impossible to help a battered spouse rebuild trust with anyone in their life or help a child get back the innocence of childhood stolen from them. I have worked countless numbers of sexual assaults involving children, many of which the offenders at the time, were victims of cases I had previously worked. I've viewed a myriad of forensic interviews that have left me nauseated. You would think that working deaths would take a larger toll on an officer, but as for me, sexual assaults and domestic violence began slowly separating me from my family. Its' hard to understand why working a case that involves terrible acts against someone, would make you lose familiarity with your family, instead of making you count yourself as blessed. Eventually, walking out of every interview or scene made me cringe at the thought of showing physical affection, which led me to be revolted by any display of intimacy.

The Greek word for the spiritual gift of mercy is *Eleeo*. It means to be patient and compassionate toward those who are suffering or afflicted. Many of us find we have this gift of concern for others' physical and spiritual needs. During our interactions with those who are hurting, we show great empathy for them throughout their trials and sufferings. Because of our positions we are alongside people over extended periods of time and sometimes, by the grace of God, we can see them through their healing process. Most officers are sensitive to the state of mind of others, the environment and circumstances that afflict them, and can genuinely detect when someone is not doing well. As Christians, we believe that God, through the Holy Spirit, blesses us with this gift of mercy, to show love to others and support them with their burdens.

We are again reminded of the gifts of grace given to us in Romans 12, and advised what to do with them, being told of mercy, *"if it is to show mercy, do it cheerfully."* This can be very difficult for some since mercy involves the idea of showing compassion, but to those who feel compelled to serve others, jollity is often found. However, it is easy to become discouraged in difficult situations, especially when our efforts to help are marginalized. Disappointed may be something other officers have become accustomed to, but for me, not being able to help those whose spirit is crushed, makes me feel as though I've failed in exercising the gifts that have been given to me. It's hard not to feel as though you've failed in some way when you can't convince a woman who is beaten time and again, into seeking help, or when the addict you've been mentoring continues to relapse. Knowing the inevitable pain a youth may continue to endure because services have failed them, or they've fallen through the cracks, takes a toll on the spirit.

Pain and suffering are unavoidable in our lives and compounded by our work. Facing death, danger and the stresses that go with them weigh heavy on the soul. Long-suffering is a quality of any seasoned officer, having or showing patience despite troubles, especially those caused by other people. Exposure to violence, horrific scenes and line of duty deaths coupled with what is often seen as a crippled justice system propagate a grief cycle that if left unchecked can lead to unbearable despair. This, along with a fractured Christian identity, leads to toxic coping mechanisms and circumstances where shame thrives.

We succeed against our despair with trust and put shame to death with grace. As Christian officers we need never view our quality of long-suffering as a badge of honor but understand that we are conquering despair through our trust in God; a trust gained believing that God runs the world by wisdom and although our view is limited, His is infinite.

The story of Job is known by most but often underplayed by many. Job is tossed about as a story of a righteous man who had everything taken away from him to test his faith. Job is a far more beautiful story than that. In his full commentary of the Bible, Matthew Henry stated the following about the Book of Job, "Were ever the being of God, His glorious attributes and perfections, His unsearchable wisdom, His irresistible power, His inconceivable glory, His inflexible justice, and His incontestable sovereignty, discoursed of with more clearness, fullness, reverence, and divine eloquence, than in this book? The creation of the world and the government of it, are here admirably described, not as matters of nice speculation, but as laying most powerful obligations upon us to fear and serve, to submit to and trust in, our Creator, owner, Lord, and ruler. Moral good and evil, virtue and vice, were never drawn more to the life (the beauty of the one and the deformity of the other) than in this book; nor the inviolable rule of God's judgment more plainly laid down, that happy are the righteous, it shall be well with them; and woe to the wicked, it shall be ill with them. These are not questions of the schools to keep the learned world in action, nor engines of state to keep the unlearned world in awe; no, it appears by this book that they are sacred truths of undoubted certainty, and which all the wise and sober part of mankind have in every age subscribed and submitted to," adding upon the book as a whole we learn "many are the afflictions of the righteous, but that when the Lord delivers them out of them all the trial of their faith will be found to praise, and honor, and glory."

Salt & Light: Being the Hands and Feet of Christ
(in a cruel and dangerous world)

~Seven~

"In His hand is the life of every creature and the breath of all mankind. Does not the ear test words as the tongue tastes food? Is not wisdom found among the aged? Does not long life bring under-standing?" ~ Job 12:10-12

In Job 38:4-7 God ask Job, as He might ask us, *"Where were you when I laid the earth's founda-tion? Tell me, if you understand. Who marked off its dimensions? Surely you know! Who stretched a measuring line across it? On what were its footings set, or who laid its cornerstone—while the morning stars sang together and all the angels shouted for joy?"* Then Job submits his will and trust to the Lord; Job 42: 1-6 *"I know that you can do all things; no purpose of yours can be thwarted. You asked, 'Who is this that obscures my plans without knowledge?' Surely I spoke of things I did not understand, things too wonderful for me to know. "You said, 'Listen now and I will speak; I will question you, and you shall answer me.' My ears had heard of you but now my eyes have seen you. Therefore, I despise myself and repent in dust and ashes."*

God had presented His servant, Job, to Satan, stating that there was no one on earth like him as he was blameless and upright, *"a man who fears God and shuns evil"* (Job 1:8). Satan in return had ques-tioned God's blessing and protection of His faithful servant and prognosticated that if that surety be challenged, Job would curse God to his face (Job 1:9-11). God then allowed everything Job had to be put under Satan's control except for his life.

The first day of Jobs affliction was indescribably
world shattering. All of Job's livestock were taken:
500 donkeys, 500 yoke of oxen, 7,000 sheep and
3,000 camels. As if it wasn't a big enough test of
someone's faith to take their livelihood, Job's ten
children (seven sons and three daughters) were
killed. Upon gaining knowledge of it all, Job wor-
shipped God. *"At this, Job got up and tore his robe
and shaved his head. Then he fell to the ground in
worship and said: "Naked I came from my mother's
womb, and naked I will depart. The Lord gave and
the Lord has taken away; may the name of the Lord
be praised"* (Job 1:20-21). In one day, Job lost everything except his faith.

Job was then afflicted with painful sores from
the soles of his feet to the crown of his head (Job
2:7) and again, did not sin but offered submission to
God. Job even called his wife foolish for questioning
why he maintained his integrity saying, *"shall we accept good from God and not trouble"* (Job 2:9)?

Job then engages in a series of conversations,
Job first questioning God, and his friends then blam-
ing his condition on him for being unrighteous, as
they offer that God operates all of existence according to rules of justice. Viewing Job and his reaction
to his suffering we see a theology begin to take
place in which Job attempts to place all responsibility on God, to the point that he wants to be as far
away from Him as possible. *"It is all the same; that
is why I say, 'He destroys both the blameless and
the wicked.' When a scourge brings sudden death,
He mocks the despair of the innocent. When a land
falls into the hands of the wicked, He blindfolds its
judges. If it is not He, then who is it?"* (9:22-24) and

then *"Are not the days of my life few? Let me alone, that I may find a little comfort"* (10:20).

Before God speaks to Job and shows him that He is not unjust or responsible for every suffering, Job comes to believe that God is the source of pain in all lives, whether righteous or wicked, a God that *"gives and takes away"* unjustly. God opens His response to Job in (34:1-3) *"Who is this that obscures my plans with words without knowledge? Brace yourself like a man; I will question you, and you shall answer me."* God shows Job that his line of thinking was broken, that in trying to make sense of tragedy he had set himself on a path of failure, a path away from God. God gives numerous examples of how Job, and we as humans, simply can't understand the works of God. *"Have you ever given orders to the morning, or shown the dawn its place, that it might take the earth by the edges and shake the wicked out of it? The earth takes shape like clay under a seal; its features stand out like those of a garment. The wicked are denied their light, and their upraised arm is broken"* (vv. 12-15); and (vv. 34-38), *"Can you raise your voice to the clouds and cover yourself with a flood of water? Do you send the lightning bolts on their way? Do they report to you, 'Here we are'? Who gives the ibis wisdom or gives the rooster understanding? Who has the wisdom to count the clouds? Who can tip over the water jars of the heavens when the dust becomes hard and the clods of earth stick together?"*

In the end, as observed previously in Job 38:4-7 and 42:1-6, Job's human wisdom is found to be insufficient and unable to explain his condition because, as humans, our view of this world and the very way it is operated is limited, whereas God's is not. When we are deep in our trials we focus on the things we can see, such as our pain instead of looking past our afflictions with the understanding that if we place our trust in God as the operator of all creation, we can gain a peace that surpasses human understanding. Job came away from his trial with a deeper sense of God's power, trusting Him more and submitting to Him.

The story of Job provides a question asked of us all, especially in law enforcement. How can we learn to trust God through our suffering? Although we may not find our bodies afflicted, the nature of our work finds us the host of a tortured soul and a mind full of unanswerable questions. 2 Corinthians 4:17-18 provides insight which validates the message given to us in Job, *"For our present troubles are small and won't last very long. Yet they produce for us a glory that vastly outweighs them and will last forever! So we don't look at the troubles we can see now; rather, we fix our gaze on things that cannot be seen. For the things we see now will soon be gone, but the things we cannot see will last forever."*

In order to trust the Lord through our trails we must accept that our life is not ours, it is God inspired and therefore our only hope lies in Him. Psalm 39:4-5 and 7 states, *"Lord, remind me how brief my time on earth will be. Remind me that my days are numbered—how fleeting my life is. You have made my life no longer than the width of my hand. My entire lifetime is just a moment to you; at best, each of us is but a breath... And so, Lord, where do I put my hope? My only hope is in you;"* and 1 Peter 5:6-7 reminds us, *"Humble yourselves, therefore, under God's mighty hand, that he may lift you up in due time. Cast all your anxiety on him because he cares for you."*

We can find in scripture multiple examples of Gods might, which should be a sure consolation as they show us that God is in control of all things. Psalm 50:1 shows His ultimate control: *"The Mighty One, God, the LORD, speaks and summons the earth from the rising of the sun to where it sets,"* and we are reminded to have patience in despair or throughout trails, especially those influenced by others. As 37:7-9 states, *"Be still before the Lord and wait patiently for Him; do not fret when people succeed in their ways, when they carry out their wicked schemes. Refrain from anger and turn from wrath; do not fret—it leads only to evil. For those who are evil will be destroyed, but those who hope in the Lord will inherit the land."* The bible warns us not to worry about tomorrow, as each day has enough trouble of its own (Matthew 6:34), and to be strong and courageous, promising us that God will be with us wherever we go (Joshua 1:9). The same trust placed in the Lord to deliver us from our darkest hours must also be employed to release us from shame.

In 2 Corinthians 12:9-10 Paul tells us that Jesus stated to him, *"My grace is sufficient for you, for my power is made perfect in weakness."* Paul concludes, *"Therefore I will boast all the more gladly about my weaknesses, so that Christ's power may rest on me. That is why, for Christ's sake, I delight in weaknesses, in insults, in hardships, in persecutions, in difficulties. For when I am weak, then I am strong."*

As Christians we are stronger when we are weak because we trust in God's grace to sustain us and rescue us from all things, including hardships brought about by our own sin. Even before Gods sacrifice of His only begotten Son, before we had a mediator to our sin and a promise of grace, God called us, showing ownership and placing us into sonship. *"But now, this is what the LORD says—He who created you, Jacob, He who formed you, Israel: "Do not fear, for I have redeemed you; I have summoned you by name; you are mine"* (Isaiah 43:1). Later Jesus said, *"Very truly I tell you, everyone who sins is a slave to sin. Now a slave has no permanent place in the family, but a son belongs to it forever. So, if the Son sets you free, you will be free indeed"* (John 8:34-36).

Paul writes of our life through the Spirit in Romans 8:1-4, *"Therefore, there is now no condemnation for those who are in Christ Jesus, because through Christ Jesus the law of the Spirit who gives life has set you free from the law of sin and death. For what the law was powerless to do because it was weakened by the flesh, God did by sending his own Son in the likeness of sinful flesh to be a sin offering. And so, He condemned sin in the flesh, in order that the righteous requirement of the law might be fully met in us, who do not live according to the flesh but according to the Spirit."* Further explaining that if we live according to the flesh we have our minds set on what the flesh desires, *"but those who live in accordance with the Spirit have their minds set on what the Spirit desires"* (Romans 8:5). Further explanation in Romans 8:10 shows although our bodies are subject to death because of sin, the Spirit will give us life because of righteousness. Paul says in verse 18, *"I consider that our present sufferings are not worth comparing with the glory that will be revealed in us,"* and continues in vv. 24-25, *"For in this hope (as we wait eagerly for our adoption to sonship) we were saved. But hope that is seen is no hope at all. Who hopes for what they already have? But if we hope for what we do not yet have, we wait for it patiently."*

It is because of this *sonship* offered to us through our desire to be in the spirit and not in the flesh that Paul asks of us in 31-32, *"If God is for us, who can be against us? He who did not spare his own Son, but gave him up for us all—how will he not also, along with him, graciously give us all things?"* He exclaims that we are more than conquers in this hope as made example in vv. 37-39, *"No, in all these things we are more than conquerors through him who loved us. For I am convinced that neither death nor life, neither angels nor demons, neither the present nor the future, nor any powers, neither height nor depth, nor anything else in all creation, will be able to separate us from the love of God that is in Christ Jesus our Lord."*

Jesus's prayers and petitions were heard because of His reverent submission. He learned obedience in His suffering and once He was made perfect, then sacrificing Himself for the new covenant, He became the source of eternal salvation for all who believe and obey Him. Placing our trust in God and our hope in His promise we allow ourselves to receive not only the grace of God but forgiveness as well.

Hebrews 8:12 states, *"For I will forgive their wickedness and will remember their sins no more,"* and follows in example, *"The blood of goats and bulls and the ashes of a heifer sprinkled on those who are ceremonially unclean sanctify them so that*

75

they are outwardly clean. How much more, then, will the blood of Christ, who through the eternal Spirit offered himself unblemished to God, cleanse our consciences from acts that lead to death, so that we may serve the living God" (Hebrews 9:13-14)! We see further examples of this hope in Ezekiel 18:20-22, *"The righteousness of the righteous will be credited to them, and the wickedness of the wicked will be charged against them. But if a wicked person turns away from all the sins they have committed and keeps all my decrees and does what is just and right, that person will surely live; they will not die. None of the offenses they have committed will be remembered against them."*

God's mercy gives us birth into a living hope though the resurrection of Jesus from the dead and an inheritance that can never perish. Shame attempts to pull us away from living like Christ by replacing our hope with fear of failure. Shame tells us that we are no better than our worst day, will never be above our transgressions and have no hope in forgiveness. We must hold to the promise of salvation through the grace of God: *"Therefore, with minds that are alert and fully sober, set your hope on the grace to be brought to you when Jesus Christ is revealed at his coming. As obedient children, do not conform to the evil desires you had when you lived in ignorance. But just as he who called you is holy, so be holy in all you do; for it is written: "Be holy, because I am holy"* (1 Peter 1:13-16).

When we forget who we are and what we believe in, God still knows. If we trust in His word and trust He is in control, we begin to understand that His love for us is truly reckless and His grace ridiculous.

There have been times when my faith felt like a fistful of sand, but I trust in the Lord and now recognize that even through our suffering, we, as servants of God, are fighting the long defeat. Justice will be served, our sufferings and sacrifices acknowledged, and sins forgotten. We must ask ourselves if we desire to live in the world or to live like Christ. Proverbs 27:19 states, *"as water reflects the face so one's life reflects the heart."* I would add you can't defeat your demons if you're still enjoying their company. Despite our appearances, we all have stories to tell and no one gets through this life unscathed.

Salt & Light: Being the Hands and Feet of Christ
(in a cruel and dangerous world)

~ Eight ~

"Blessed is the one who perseveres under trial because, having stood the test, that person will receive the crown of life that the Lord has promised to those who love him." ~ James 1:12

Seven words culminate one of the most loaded questions law enforcement professionals could ever field. The average citizen would never know and could never fully understand the honest answer to this question, and I'd say fairly some officers can't either. "How much does all that stuff weigh?" In layman's terms the answer is quite simple, thirty pounds. The answer seems to be enough for most to go on about how they couldn't wear our gear all day or talk at length about all the back problems they would have as a result of carrying such a weight for an extended period of time. People see a vest and badge. Civilians see a duty belt with handcuffs, firearm, baton, magazines, Taser, keys, and flashlight. They are unable to weigh the things left unseen, the things we carry on the inside. Sadly, the truth is thirty pounds isn't that hard to carry and an honest scale of the weight of our service is hard to term.

Every day officers carry their communities. As Christian officers we not only carry the burdens of the people we encounter but we feel the weight on their spirit. We find ourselves invited into some of the worst times of the worst days of people's lives. It's a very intimate relationship whether realized or not. Empathizing with victims we often share in their grief as they do and in the worst of cases, may carry it with us our entire life.

I found it very hard finding a place to start this chapter. Up until now, my faults have not been something easily or openly spoken about, even with friends and loved ones. In fact, most people didn't even know until now and still won't if they don't read this. Thinking of a way to explain some of the dark places I've been as a civilian is hard but as a peace officer, how do you even begin? Painting a picture that has been so tightly held to the vest is near impossible, and even if we wanted to, fear generally keeps us from fully opening up and letting go.

"Hello, my name is Matt... and I'm an alcoholic."

As horrible and insensitive as it sounds, had it not been for my faith in God, I might have suck-started a Glock a long time ago. I was living a life that led to death and what's worse, I felt I deserved it. I lost control, lost myself and cashed my days in 750ml at a time. Now I never drank at work or before work. I was never drunk at work nor did I stay fall-down drunk during my off time, but I don't believe that being an alcoholic is based on how much you drink or when you drink, it's based on desire. There's a lot of things that led to the desire and caused me to lose sight of God's will, but I can articulate the sum of them with one word—fear.

I had come to a place in my career that left me feeling empty, worthless, scared and vulnerable. I couldn't shut down—my hypervigilance was constant and I had no enjoyment. I felt as though my world was going to collapse all at once. I was suffering from night terrors, flashbacks, sleepwalking, and depression. It's not easy living a nightmare no one can see and is even harder to explain. Developing a

drinking problem was easy, as I had dealt with se-
vere chronic pain for many years, and the weight of
my work only amplified it. I found myself like the
wicked, stumbling blocks put in front of me by my
own hand, trying to explain spiritual hardships by
earthly means. I convinced myself that since Jesus
had suffered for me, in order to earn grace, I too
had to suffer. Mental and physical pain was something I had to bear on my own. This was my punishment for being a sinner; I had to atone for the life I
was living and things I had done. I failed to lean on
the word of God and listened to my own selfish and
ignorant advice based on personal experience.

I never learned to grieve properly, and in turn,
exercised no healthy outlet for my anger or suffering. I let shame take precedence over mercy, and
although I fought long and hard not to let bitterness
into my heart, it found its way in through grief. I si-
lently battled a personal spiritual conflict every day.
As strange as it sounds, I was afraid to let go of the
pain. Convinced that holding onto it was the only
control I had, I found the reality of peace nonexist-
ent. The saying, "misery loves company," became
truth and when despair became my companion, I began to hate myself.

Holding on to my pain made me emotionally
empty. I find difficulty in clarifying how I could sim-
ultaneously feel so many emotions, and yet, not be
able to exhibit them. My anxiety manifested itself in
anger, and although I attempted my best to hold it
together, I was very aware that there was something
dark inside of me. Crippling my identity as a father,
husband, and friend, I fell into a pattern of going
through the motions. I was far beyond stoic; I was an
affectionless shell. Intimacy was a mere after

thought with my wife, and I started detesting physical contact of any nature. I got to a point where I couldn't even embrace my children with a simple hug.

Feeling completely worthless, numbing my grief with alcohol became the answer. When I drank I could turn off the officer for a little while, at least that's what I thought. Consuming alcohol became the only way I could let go of any grief, even though doing so caused more. I began living my life looking through the glass, drinking down bottles with shame; four fingers poured neat and left incomplete. Every morning I pulled myself out of bed and stared at my almost colorless face. I prayed the day would go by fast and begged that I wouldn't have to deal with problematic people. I was tired, drained, and didn't want any more drama than necessary. I just wanted to get home, pop the cork and try to escape. I hated everything about being a sluggish drunk and was disgusted with myself.

The daily activities were always the same. Go to work, solve people's problems, seem so solid, and in the end, feel unfit to live. I wasn't suicidal, never have been, but I was ashamed. I felt horrible for how I was living, what my wife and children had to see. They knew I was better than that and I knew it too. I caught myself looking at my reflection a lot as if I could reach myself somehow and stop the damage but continued to suffocate that consideration with drunkenness. I walked in continuous circles trying to work off the anxiety and although I wanted to, I never could express to my wife how I felt. I was scared she would never be able to understand. How exactly do you tell your spouse that you don't want to play with your kids because when you look at them, all you see are the victims, or that the officer in you is telling you not to get attached, so you can *"do your job"* should something happen? I really wanted children and had felt so blessed to receive them. My wife and I tried for seven years before we had our first, my son, Matson. All those years I begged and pleaded with God to bless us with a child. I told my wife over and over again to just have faith, and here I was trying my best to avoid developing a relationship with my son and daughter.

On really bad nights, I ended up drinking until I passed out. I found sleep but no rest, although it was better than the images I saw time and again. I have seen things I wished I'd never seen, and still do. They are as real and vivid today as they were when they occurred.

Alcoholism is lonely enough but the effects of my depression, anxiety, and cumulative stress made me feel completely cut off. Sometimes I felt like I was dead, and nobody knew it but me. I had many moments of clarity, awe inspiring moments of godly sorrow in which I observed the sad being I had become. I knew I would eventually lose everything, understood the steps I needed to take to change, and I drank even harder to get rid of that realization. Sober I was scared, constantly on alert and the triggers were endless. It was as easy as walking into a new room, getting a strange vibe, catching a smell, and as hard as I tried, I couldn't turn it off. Sometimes I couldn't differentiate between real life and my nightmares. It felt like at any moment, something horrible was going to happen, and there was nothing I would be able to do about it.

I know this happens to normal people as well, but as officers, every day we go to work we are walking right back into the environment that caused the issue in the first place. The routine becomes exhausting. Normal people drive down the road, they know where they are and how to get where they're going. They see landmarks. Places they've stopped before along the way, gone to eat, been to a garage sale. Officers do the same thing except we see the body on the side of the road, the horrible wreck we worked, the houses we've been to repeatedly for the abuse of children or worked a sexual assault, the place where you fought for your life, or the heart-rending scene of a suicide. The scenes never go away, the images are always there. Every day is the day it happened, and they just keep adding up. The toll each scene takes on you adds up as well and remind you of how fragile life is and how evil people can be.

I personally lived in constant fear that my son was going to be killed. Every morning I walked out the door, I thought it would be the last day I saw him and chose not to look back. Fighting that certainty, his death inevitably became my mind's reality. Just seeing my son triggered my anxiety. He would come running toward me, smiling and full of life, and an emotional wall would go up immediately. *"Fight or flight Matt. Lock down those emotions, treat them like victims, do your job."* I perfected this restrained tactic, effectively policing my family. I felt that any minute, God might choose to test what little faith I was holding onto and take them all away from me.

Besides the driving urge to drink, when I got off work, I would stay later just so they would be gone when I got home. Staying away from my family almost made life seem easier to pretend they were

84

never there, than to admit I might have to deal with their loss. This also gave me time to get a few glasses in, relax, and let a little bit of the fear fade before they got home. I wasn't much use to them then anyway but at least I wasn't looking at ghosts.

I am far from righteous, but the example of Job still stands. Job, although righteous in the eyes of God, had come to a flawed view that God was unjust. It's not that Job didn't believe in God, he was just mistaken in his judgement of Him, and misinterpreted grief with human logic. I had done the same thing. I had misinterpreted my grief. I didn't think God was unjust or not there, in fact I knew He was there. I had just alleviated my faith to the point I forgot I had access to Him, and felt if I did, then I didn't deserve to.

As police officers, the idea of control is in our nature. Control is something that we must always aspire to. Every situation we walk into demands that we govern the circumstances. As Christian police officers we need to learn how to let go, and place our trust in God, not ourselves. I was raised in a Christian household, I believed strongly in God, but because of fear, I failed to develop a borderless trust with Him. Despite the blinders I wore, God continued reaching out to me and though I was able to hear Him all along, one day, I was finally willing.

My children were actively participating in Wednesday night youth services, and truly enjoyed it. One day, my wife did as any other wives do, and advised me that we were going to service that coming Sunday. I was actually excited. That Sunday was the first time, we as a family, went to service together. I remembered having a feeling of hope, something I hadn't felt for a while. I never asked her what compelled her to push the issue; I just know her persistence saved my life.

One Sunday we were in church singing. I don't recall the sermon or the song playing, but I do recall the voice. This deeply sorrowful feeling overtook me, like a question in my soul, "will I ever find peace?" At that moment, I felt my answer. Yes, felt it. Have you ever heard something that changes your whole attitude? How about hearing something and your world changes? One voice, one word, "surrender." I nearly fell to the ground in awe! At that very moment I was filled with so much joy, and began praying, asking God to help me let go of my pain, and offering the suffering I was holding on to up to Him. I finally saw a path for hope, finally tasted solace.

Philippians 4:7 says, *"And the peace of God, which surpasses all understanding, will guard your hearts and minds in Christ Jesus."* The peace of God is amazing, and as stated, is unexplainable. Obtaining that peace requires trust, and I was far from full submission.

~ Nine ~

"Very truly I tell you, no one can see the king-dom of God unless they are born again." ~ John 3:3

I never knew such peace could reside amongst so much chaos until I heard that voice say "surrender." A little weight was lifted that day, but the battle within me raged ahead. I saw that my fear was as simple a thing to conquer as letting go and letting God. I just couldn't do it. You would think as a Christian, something as simple as saying, "thy will be done," would be an easy undertaking, when in fact it was the scariest thing I had ever done, and in all honesty, I still found it a hard truth to accept *His* will and say, "it is well with my soul." There were things that I was not willing to let go of yet. Things that were obviously never going to be within my con-trol, thoughts mostly, but it scared the hell out of me to even begin entertaining the idea of relinquish-ing full control to God, as if control was ever mine to give anyway. Even though I started down the path to forgiveness, fear kept me from completely surren-dering to God.

My fear that my son was going to die only got worse and started to include my pregnant wife and youngest daughter. A steady stream of nightmares, and unbelievable anxiety fueled the belief that I was being led into a time of testing, and I was going to be left here all alone with what little strength I could muster to carry me through. The more I tried to let go of that fear, the more it seemed that God was trying to prepare me, that something was going to happen, and I was going to have to accept it. I

just wanted all the sorrow and hurt I felt to go away
and believed God was able to do that.

I remembered Jesus said, *"With man this is impossible, but with God all things are possible"* (Matthew 19:26). I told myself that nothing was impossible for God, but God didn't want me to remember
He could do all things, He wanted me to accept that
even if He didn't, He was still my only hope.

In Daniel 3:17-18 Shadrach, Meshach and Abed-
nego are about to be killed and say, *"if we are
thrown into the blazing furnace, the God we serve is
able to deliver us from it, and he will deliver us
from Your Majesty's hand. But even if he does not,
we want you to know, Your Majesty that we will not
serve your gods or worship the image of gold you
have set up."*

Now that is a faith that leaves the grave behind.
God wanted me to have that faith. More importantly
He wanted me to have that relationship of trust.
That trust did not develop overnight. The feelings of
death looming around each turn didn't go away, the
visions of interring my son didn't disappear, the
nightmares of not being able to save him didn't stop,
but God didn't stop either. I consistently told myself, "No matter what happens, no matter what God
chooses to do, there is hope and it is in Him." Then
one night I believed.

Having yet another horrible night filled with the
same fears, anxiety, and coping methods, I became
completely worn out. I told God, "I give up." I was
done living in constant fear; done trying to keep and
carry the suffering of others or myself, done trying
to contain my mess of an existence and willing to
accept the outcome, whatever it may be. I prayed to

God about my pain, about my son and family, and all my suffering saying, "thy will be done." I meant it, I was bitter, but I meant it. That night was the last time I consumed alcohol. I left a note the next morning telling my wife that she wouldn't have to worry about me anymore, or my drinking for that matter, and went to work. I was completely spent. There was no fight left in me to go against God's plans, whatever they may be. My promise to her was halfhearted but God ensured it.

While at work I collapsed from a punishing pain. I had experienced two similar episodes prior to this one, both of which kept me in bed for two days and left me in pain for two weeks, but this was near unbearable. I stripped my duty gear off and laid on the floor in the police department. My chief drove me to the emergency room, and the staff quickly went to work attempting to figure out what was wrong. The pain would not relent and continued crushing any hope that it would pass. I have never felt anything that came close to its level, and I've had a completely degenerated disc. This was a different kind of pain, a harrowing one.

I didn't want my chief to call my wife until something was figured out about my condition but after being persistent in the matter, he did. She in turn had my mother and father go to the hospital. Don't take me wrong, I love that they wanted to be there for me, but I didn't want my family seeing me in such distress, and I was relatively embarrassed about the situation.

The doctor told me I wasn't going anywhere for a while, put me in a room, finally gave me some good drugs, and I rolled over, passing into darkness. There's something to be said about what a bad time you must be having when you go to sleep with clothes on and wake up coughing vomit out of your lungs into a cup while wearing a hospital gown. I don't remember anything before that unfortunate moment. Apparently, I had thrown up and aspirated it. Later, my wife told me that I was lucky to be a side sleeper. Blessed is the word I thought of.

I was admitted to the hospital for four days because of my pancreas, which, in turn, put me out of work nearly two weeks. They said the cause of the issue could be a combination of variables, but I knew the reasons. Eating correctly, if at all, didn't happen often. I couldn't keep most meals down until the afternoon. There were frequently days I couldn't even keep water on my stomach. Throwing up had become a morning ritual and a staple in my evening activities. With two prior episodes (now knowing what they were) and the current worse one, I was told that chances of developing chronic pancreatitis were very probable and would be most definite, should I continue to drink.

That was it for me. That was it for my wife as well. The threats she made that time were very real. I'm a stubborn man and sometimes made very ill-informed decisions but I'm not stupid. I knew she meant it; I knew she'd leave. I finally believed her and I wasn't going to test her. She had stayed with me through everything; she had been punished just as I was punishing myself. She deserved better. Winning that woman's love was no easy feat. I worked long and hard for that, worked even harder to keep it and now I wasn't going to lose her over one more sip of liquid folly. I also decided that even if I did suffer another attack and missed work over it, it would not be due to alcohol.

I started being a little more open about the way I had been feeling for a long time and some of the effects of it. I stopped drinking completely, cut down my tobacco intake substantially and slowly started laying down the weight of my burdens at the foot of the Cross.

Make no mistake, it was no instant fix. Reestablishing my spiritual strength was tough. The first month was the hardest, but started getting easier about two weeks in. I noticed when I came home I was finding no enjoyment. I wasn't scared like I had been, but I wasn't happy either. In fact, I didn't really feel anything at all. I didn't want to watch shows, didn't really want to move, and didn't know what to do. I just sat there feeling useless until my family got home, or I went to bed. Not drinking left a huge hole in my evening activities, a hole I started slowly filling with the word of God. Placing my trust in God a little at a time, day by day I started feeling as though I could actually control my anxiety, feelings of fear, look past my faults, and look toward a new life led the right way. And I did.

My demons didn't go away, but it became much easier to live with them. When you surrender yourself to God, life becomes less complicated. There are less worrisome hours spent on needless wonderings. I still have issues, but I see them head on instead of repressing them. I still have some of the same fears, like losing my son, still have incredible moments of anxiety that rush on without warning, but I allow myself to feel them and allow God to see me through them instead of trying to make them fade away through destructive means.

Allowing God to fix me helped open my eyes and set me on a path to reach my full potential both as a man and officer to be a servant of Christ. It also drove me to tell others of the hope we have and what kind of servants we can be, as I'm sure I was not the only one out of 750,000 sworn officers to ever feel the way I did. There is hope and once we learn to bridge the division we may face as Christian officers at a personal level, we can again focus on being true servants, showing physical acts of love, and attempt to fix the spiritual division this nation and our communities experience.

~ Ten ~

"As a father has compassion on his children, so the LORD has compassion on those who fear him."
~ Psalm 103:13

As previously stated division, desire, despair, and fear keep us from fully accepting the love of God, and in turn, showing it. Division between a community and at the personal level, our desires to be in control or to only influence things in our lives that place our trust in ourselves, sinking despair and grief that lie and tell us we can never be any better or that we are not worthy of the love of God. All these things keep us from achieving servanthood in the example of Christ. In the end, fear is the master of them all and remains the main opponent of surrender.

To ultimately know God, His love and to serve like Christ, we must meet His expectation of that love which requires us to surrender everything to Him. Not just some parts of our lives but all of it. We surrender our understanding, our trust, and our lives to God, in order that we may fully lean on the power of God to give us strength, guidance, and the salvation of His grace. Giving up complete control, especially as a police officer, is no easy task.

I'm sure if some of us examined ourselves we would find that our desires and fears so dominate us that we are unable to avoid sin. And, although we attempt to serve God and our works outwardly appear good, our sinful intentions affect all our actions and therefore fail to glorify God.

Salvation requires we not only be knowledgeable of our faith but trust in God's promise to save, understanding that God's grace is sufficient. Ezekiel 18:21-22 states, *"But if a wicked person turns away from all the sins they have committed and keeps all my decrees and does what is just and right, that person will surely live; they will not die. None of the offenses they have committed will be remembered against them."*

We are reminded again throughout the Book of Psalms of where to place our trust. *"God is our refuge and strength, an ever-present help in trouble. Therefore, we will not fear, though the earth give way and the mountains fall into the heart of the sea though its waters roar and foam and the mountains quake with their surging"* (Psalm 46:1-3). Psalm 46:10-11 states, *"He says, "Be still, and know that I am God; I will be exalted among the nations, I will be exalted in the earth. The Lord Almighty is with us; the God of Jacob is our fortress."* And, *"Yes, my soul, find rest in God; my hope comes from him. Truly he is my rock and my salvation; he is my fortress, I will not be shaken"* (Psalm 62:5-6). These passages tell us about the omnipresent nature of God and remind us of the importance to accept forgiveness.

When we accept forgiveness from God, we remove blind spots in our lives that have kept us from seeing the full extent of the work we can do as Christian police officers. Understanding that we are sinful ourselves, and yet, worthy of the grace of God, should only educate us more in that we have chosen a profession called upon to help others. And that should prompt us to cover transgressions against us with the same amount of mercy.

Sometimes we need to be reminded that it is not just the duty of our preachers, pastors or other clergy members prevalent in our lives to share the gospel, but as Christians, it is our personal duty to also share the gospel. We must also be reminded that the gospel of grace is intended for everyone to hear, as the salvation of God is not limited to any sect. God gives us the tools required to deliver this message in our personal day to day lives, and through the work we do.

As officers it's easy to get in the habit of not sharing the word of God. Some of us fear that we may be called out or persecuted for allowing our convictions and discipleship to be viewed while following the mission statement of any department or agency that employs us. Some people will complain about an officer for any reason, and sometimes sharing the message of God while attempting to help someone will be that very reason.

Romans 1:16-17 states, *"For I am not ashamed of the gospel, for it is the power of God for salvation to everyone who believes, to the Jew first and also to the Greek. For in it the righteousness of God is revealed from faith for faith, as it is written, 'The righteous shall live by faith.'"*

It is our duty as members of the body of Christ to share the same gospel of grace that gives us salvation with everyone. Not just when it's convenient but even more so when it's not. In moving away from our comfort zone and trusting in God to sustain and guide us through His word, we not only gain a freedom that allows our faith to grow but God's Kingdom grows as well.

As officers, when we demonstrate fairness and compassion, we in turn teach fairness and compassion. I believe we do this through learning humility, and knowing unwaveringly that redemption and salvation are offered to everyone no matter their sin. Granted, some make the choice to ignore grace, but police officers can still attempt to show that hope through our actions, living and working in Gods image.

Romans 5:6-8 states, *"You see, at just the right time, when we were still powerless, Christ died for the ungodly. Very rarely will anyone die for a righteous person, though for a good person someone might possibly dare to die. But God demonstrates his own love for us in this: While we were still sinners, Christ died for us."*

Ungodly is defined as denying or disobeying God, being impious, irreligious or contrary to moral law. Similar definitions describe ungodly as sinful, wicked or immoral, and living ungodly lives of self-obsession, lust and pleasure.

Christ died for us, even in our ungodly state, to demonstrate God's love. What are we that He cares for us if we can't even care for each other? The same fairness and compassion that helps to define God's love should be utilized by each of us in order to show it.

The simple way to term compassion is that we connect with those who are in pain. This is obviously something that most of us as officers are good at, although if we're honest, we probably tend to judge whether we are willing to extend that compassion to everyone.

1 Samuel 16:7 says *"People look at the outward appearance, but the Lord looks at the heart."*

We must recognize the barriers we set that keep us from showing Christ-like compassion such as the bitterness that comes along with our cynicism, our suspicions we have of people, and the irritation and frustration we encounter from repeated circumstances.

Ephesians 4:29-31 states, *"Do not let any unwholesome talk come out of your mouths, but only what is helpful for building others up according to their needs, that it may benefit those who listen. And do not grieve the Holy Spirit of God, with whom you were sealed for the day of redemption. Get rid of all bitterness, rage and anger, brawling and slander, along with every form of malice."*

When we feel like we can't extend that courtesy, as it was given to us, we should pray for God to guide our hearts to be *"kind and tenderhearted"* as stated in Ephesians 4:32, so even when we are dealing with that same offender or victim in any circumstance, we can show sympathy.

We are called in Romans 12:15 to 'rejoice with those who rejoice and mourn with those who mourn.' That compassion should not only be shared with our brothers and sisters in Christ but with all who connect to us on the human level, lest we forget Psalm 145:8-9. *"The Lord is gracious and compassionate, slow to anger and rich in love. The Lord is good to all; he has compassion on all he has made."*

Most people would have you believe that compassion is a sign of weakness, when in fact it is a display of strength. Jesus, being of God, and setting the example of faithful service, showed compassion for sinners, not that He was tolerant or even accepted their depraved nature, but to show them an opportunity to repent and turn back to God. In Matthew 9:10-13 Jesus was having dinner at Matthew's house. The scripture tells us that many tax collectors and sinners came and ate with Him and His disciples.

His disciples were asked by the Pharisees, *"Why does your teacher eat with tax collectors and sinners?"* Jesus responded, *"It is not the healthy who need a doctor, but the sick. But go and learn what this means: 'I desire mercy, not sacrifice.' For I have not come to call the righteous, but sinners."*

Further, Colossians 3:12-14 shows us that compassion is among the qualities of God's people. *"Therefore, as God's chosen people, holy and dearly loved, clothe yourselves with compassion, kindness, humility, gentleness and patience. Bear with each other and forgive one another if any of you has a grievance against someone. Forgive as the Lord forgave you. And over all these virtues put on love, which binds them all together in perfect unity."*

As Christian police officers we should view compassion not only as our duty, but as a positive, natural reflection of our lives in Christ, a virtue in need of constant development, so we can be of better use in the lives of others. When we devote our life to God and place His interests first, true compassion comes naturally, and we begin to see His preeminence. When we seek knowledge outside of our own and reflect on God's direction and answers to bring guidance to others through His word, we bring them closer to God. We bring ourselves closer to Him as well. The sorrows we endure help strengthen our character and benefit us in our work toward others, so we can show them a way through their troubles, because we too have gone through them.

In Romans 12:1 we are called to be a *"living sacrifice"* in the view of God's mercy, then being *"holy and pleasing to God"* as *"this is your true and proper worship."* In Thessalonians 5:14-15 we are urged to warn those who are idle and disruptive, encourage the disheartened, help the weak, and be patient with everyone making sure that nobody pays back wrong for wrong, but that we always strive to do what is good for each other and for everyone else. These embodiments of compassion guide us and others to learn genuine empathy and gain a sincere understanding of the passion God has for us and His will for us to share it.

Intercessory prayer is one of the ways we can show our love and sympathy. Prayer is helpful, if not needed, to develop compassion and exercise kindness especially toward those we find hard to tolerate. Intercessory prayer is praying for others or pleading another's case. The act can be defined as holy, believing, persevering prayer whereby someone pleads with God on behalf of another or others who desperately need God's intervention. What is great is that Christ has already given us the ultimate illustration of it since He is the mediator between God and man (1Timothy 2:5).

Hebrews 7:25 states, *"Therefore He is also able to save to the uttermost those who come to God through Him, since He always lives to make intercession for them."* We also see this example in Romans 8:34, *"It is Christ who died, and furthermore is also risen, who is even at the right hand of God, who also makes intercession for us."*

I urge you to attempt the following. Whenever you feel distain for a situation you are dealing with, or a person with whom you come into contact with regularly, pray over it and pray for them, that God may guide their hearts and present a solution. Practice intercessory prayer for a week to see the difference it makes. A few days of waking up, giving praise and thanks to God, and then praying for others instead of yourself, will definitely change your outlook on life. Praying for others will also change your whole attitude toward the task you perform at work. If something is important enough for you to pour all your time and effort into it, then surely it is important enough to pray about as well.

Although Jesus serves as our mediator in Heaven, we remember that He prayed for us while on Earth. *"My prayer is not for them alone. I pray also for those who will believe in me through their message, that all of them may be one, Father, just as you are in me and I am in you. May they also be in us so that the world may believe that you have sent me. I have given them the glory that you gave me, that they may be one as we are one—I in them and you in me—so that they may be brought to complete unity. Then the world will know that you sent me and have loved them even as you have loved me. Father, I want those you have given me to be with me where I am, and to see my glory, the glory you have given me because you loved me before the creation of the world. Righteous Father, though the world does not know you, I know you, and they know that you have sent me. I have made you known to them and will continue to make you known in order that the love you have for me may be in them and that I myself may be in them (John 17 20-26)."*

What a beautiful prayer and exact representation of how we should pray for and love each other; that we may know God and make Him known to others. Showing compassion and praying over those you arrest or find vexing, will impact your life; moreover, it might change theirs.

Compassion or wanting to relieve someone's suffering, comes from empathy, the outward showing of
a connection to one's suffering. Empathy is gained
through pity, first acknowledging others suffering,
and then sympathy, showing you care. 2 Corinthians
1:3-4 says, *"Praise be to the God and Father of our
Lord Jesus Christ, the Father of compassion and the
God of all comfort, who comforts us in all our troubles, so that we can comfort those in any trouble
with the comfort we ourselves receive from God."*

The comfort God gives as the *"Father of compassion"* is copious and able to comfort in *"any
trouble,"* not just some situations. Compassion is also meant to be given with the same eagerness it is
received. Although in this passage Paul is speaking to
the Church it is understood through God's grace that
"those" in trouble does not simply refer to the
members of the congregation, but to all on whom
God has compassion and Psalm 145:9 again states
that is everything and everyone. *"The Lord is good
to all; he has compassion on all he has made."*

Paul described their persecutions to the Church,
stating they were under great pressure, far beyond
their ability to endure, to the point they despaired
life itself, adding, *"Indeed, we felt we had received
the sentence of death* (2 Corinthians 1:8-9)." Paul
showed that patient endurance is gained though
hope placed in God. *"Our conscience testifies that
we have conducted ourselves in the world, and especially in our relations with you, with integrity and
godly sincerity. We have done so, relying not on
worldly wisdom but on God's grace* (2 Corinthians
1:12)."

A further example of that grace is found in Hebrews 4:15-16. The text states, *"For we do not have*

a high priest who cannot sympathize with our weaknesses, but One who has been tempted in all things as we are, yet without sin." Jesus, although without sin, was tempted and led through testing just as we are. It is because of this fact that we have a mediator with God who can show sympathy toward our weaknesses. The text concludes, *"Therefore let us draw near with confidence to the throne of grace, so that we may receive mercy and find grace to help in time of need."*

If we are to accept that Jesus, who intercedes for us, operates with the compassion of God and sympathizes with our condition in order that we may *"receive mercy and find grace,"* then it is essential to accept that we must display that same mercy and grace, when needed for the benefit of others.

In the parable of the unmerciful servant we find one narration of the mercy all of us as Christians are called to show each other. The master questioned his servant in Matthew 18:33 stating, *"shouldn't you have had mercy on your fellow servant just as I had on you?"* God asks that same question of us. We are told in God's word to be merciful because He was merciful to us. I know many police officers recall Matthew 5:9, *"Blessed are the peacemakers, for they will be called children of God,"* but just two verses before that in 5:7 we find, *"Blessed are the merciful, for they will be shown mercy."* A daily walk through the Eight Beatitudes of Jesus makes a great checklist while fielding calls for service.

In Galatians 1:6-10 Paul states, *"I am astonished that you are so quickly deserting the one who called you to live in the grace of Christ and are turning to a different gospel—which is really no gospel at all. Evidently some people are throwing you into confu-*

sion and are trying to pervert the gospel of Christ. But even if we or an angel from heaven should preach a gospel other than the one we preached to you, let them be under God's curse! As we have already said, so now I say again: If anybody is preaching to you a gospel other than what you accepted, let them be under God's curse! Am I now trying to win the approval of human beings, or of God? Or am I trying to please people? If I were still trying to please people, I would not be a servant of Christ."

Paul was telling the Galatians that they had left the Gospel of Grace and began preaching another. That they believed they were saved by grace through faith, but victory could only be achieved through a different gospel, a gospel of works, speaking of grace as just a *"message."* Grace is no mere message or talking point in relation to the Gospel, grace *is* the Gospel. In Acts 20:24 Paul states, *"But none of these things move me; nor do I count my life dear to myself, so that I may finish my race with joy, and the ministry which I received from the Lord Jesus, to testify to the gospel of the grace of God."* Paul again speaks of this grace and mercy in Ephesians 2:4-5, *"But because of his great love for us, God, who is rich in mercy, made us alive with Christ even when we were dead in transgressions—it is by grace you have been saved."* The ugliest truth of our humanity contains the beauty of its saving grace; that we all, at some point, have failed to recognize the love of God.

The grace of God is unmerited, unearned favor that is not produced by works but empowers our works to further God's Kingdom. Jesus took on the cross and our sin, so that all could take on His righteousness. Furthermore, Jesus died the death we all deserve for us to achieve a promise of life earned through His blood. Unmerited, unearned favor! Can you tell me who is undeserving of that Grace?

~ Eleven ~

"Let us consider how to stir up one another to love and good works, not neglecting to meet together... but encourage one another." ~ Hebrews 10:24-25

Observing past scripture—compassion, kindness, humility, gentleness, and patience are all bound together in perfect unity by love. Since all virtue at its core can be considered sacrifice, then sacrifice itself is love in action. In exercising any virtue, we sacrifice something. We give something up so that someone else might benefit. In order that our sacrifice is selfless we need to redefine our definition of the term. Christians should not view sacrifice as giving up something but as offering up with love. We also need to retrain ourselves on the difference between sacrifice and moral duties.

Our moral duty is to give all we can past our own needs to those in our care and those we love, but sacrifice is giving all we can past our own needs to those whose care we are not charged with. Our sense of value must be placed beyond what actions are only beneficial to us in the end. If we are only acting so that we or others may remember our best actions, then we label ourselves immoral in terms of sacrifice. I will not go as far as pushing altruism as the defining principal of sacrifice, given the belief held by some that the advantages it brings to others must result in disadvantages to the giver. Altruism might also require the surrender of something of greater value for the sake of something of less value, or require our virtue be measured by the degree we betray our values, mandating we give to enemies in stead of those we love. While I believe it is a great moral practice and shines a light on the path of sacrifice, I do not think altruism is the sole example, especially if one believes the actor must be disadvantaged in the end. If an officer operates on a foundation of faith in God and the promise of salvation, how could that servant ever be disadvantaged due to sacrifice?

As previously mentioned in 1 Corinthians 13 we were taught the facets of love. The scripture did not tell us what love *is* but told us what love *does*. The evilest people on earth know the virtues of love; they just choose not to put those virtues into practice. Even Christian officers can find love easier to appreciate than it is to apply. Selfishness, pride, and jealousy continue to divide communities in a culture that measures others by their gifts. In order to give selflessly, we must learn to exercise a love that is given without considering the worth of the person receiving it. Too often we fall victim to our emotions rather than meditating on God's word and praying for the characteristics needed to overcome situations we find too burdensome for us. If we aspire to be servants of God's will, we must employ the characteristics of love daily. Our works must be good willed, unpretentious, and humble. We must honor others, never being egocentric, but mild tempered and forgiving. Always protect, display trust and constant hope in God, while being truthful and demonstrating perseverance knowing that love never fails.

What good is our work if we don't implement the love described above to those we serve? What does that say about the way we view our moral duties? It surely wouldn't say we are servants of sacrifice. We

operate within a job field that ultimately could require our lives. At any moment and for any reason,
we could lose everything. Whether this occurs in an
effort to save another person's life, or in the course
of affecting the "routine" stop for a traffic violation,
the sad truth is that this reality for some of us is easier to accept, and live out, than it is for us to show
love to those who truly need it most. Some officers
have convinced themselves that since there is a possibility of ultimate sacrifice, they are fulfilling their
moral duties and obligations as Christian police officers, by the simple action of showing up for duty.
It's not just what you give in the end that matters,
it's what you give in every moment, why you give,
and whether or not love is the root of those actions.

If I haven't lost you yet, this could quite possibly
be the paragraph in which I do. Do not aspire to be
called a hero but instead desire to display the selflessness of one. The word "hero" in our profession
has been overused and under-defined. In this writ-
er's opinion, we as a collective, have found ourselves so quick to defend an institution, even when
faced with wrong, that our culture has attempted to
perpetuate hero status to anyone wearing a uniform.

Are we not lying to ourselves if we say we would
lay down our lives for a total stranger but can't be
bothered to show compassion to those less fortunate
or to our enemies? Being a hero requires one being
put under extraordinary circumstances, and then
showing a complete lack of regard for ones being to
perform actions that go beyond the moral duties entrusted to them. Anyone at any time can become a
hero, but as police officers, we are given a stage to
show our selflessness daily. We can take the abilities
God has given us and the powers entrusted to us by

the people to show the selfless love that heroes give, so we can be seen as humble servants.

In a collection of lectures entitled *Signs Amid the Rubble: The Purposes of God in Human History*, Lesslie Newbigin writes that progress depends on men's will to direct greater powers to good or evil ends, advising that, *"the human will retains its paradoxical character as being capable at the same time of the most glorious heroism and of the basest evil,"* and adding, *"the greater a man's growth in power, the deeper the possible disaster."*

Thomas Carlyle wrote, *"Adversity is sometimes hard upon a man; but for one man who can stand prosperity, there are a hundred that will stand adversity* (Heroes and Hero Worship (1840), Lecture V).*"* Carlyle is stating that as difficult as the world may be, hardship is often easier for man to handle than success, following a narrative that gaining wealth or power tends to corrupt men's nature.

Romans 15:1-2 outlines moral duty stating, *"We who are strong ought to bear with the failings of the weak and not to please ourselves. Each of us should please our neighbors for their good, to build them up."*

God calls us to show love and be of service to one another, creating in each of us specific gifts and a unique possibility to contribute to His Kingdom. By putting our faith into practice, through our work we can begin to view all our efforts as having value. All work done for the glory of God lasts forever.

Newbigin again outlines selfless commitment to the continued progress of God's Kingdom and illustrates the immutability of love in action stating, *"Every faithful act of service, every honest labor to make the world a better place, which seemed to have been forever lost and forgotten in the rubble of history, will be seen on that day [at the final resurrection] to have contributed to the perfect fellowship of God's kingdom.... All who committed their work in faithfulness to God will be by Him raised up to share in the new age, and will find that their labor was not lost, but that it has found its place in the completed kingdom."* Newbigin continues, *"Whoever is faithfully seeking, whether as an engineer, an economist, a politician, a craftsman, a teacher or a friend, to overcome that which militates against true human fellowship even though all the visible results of his labor perish before his eyes, it is no more lost than he is himself if he dies in faith,"* and *"The outward implements of fellowship will perish; but in the day when the perfected people of God are gathered together in the fellowship of the Kingdom, he will know that his work was not in vain."* Newbigin's vision is not just that of a hopeful man but an affirmation of the word of God and translation of the very testament we are given in scripture.

Throughout 1 Corinthians 15 Paul writes of our victory over death through the resurrection, and the importance of staying in faith and producing works of faith. Paul says in vv. 30-34, *"And as for us, why do we endanger ourselves every hour? I face death every day—yes, just as surely as I boast about you in Christ Jesus our Lord. If I fought wild beasts in Ephesus with no more than human hopes, what have I gained? If the dead are not raised, 'Let us eat and drink, for tomorrow we die.'"*

This was a testament to the persecution and trials he had suffered because he believed in the resurrection of Christ from the dead. Paul advances to the feebleness of death over us or our works stating, *"O death, where is thy sting? O grave, where is thy victory?"* in vs. 55 and then, *"Therefore, my dear brothers and sisters, stand firm. Let nothing move you. Always give yourselves fully to the work of the Lord, because you know that your labor in the Lord is not in vain,"* vs. 58.

However, we are reminded in Ephesians 2:8-9 that it is by grace, a gift from God, that we are saved through faith (as Paul described) and not the results of our works *"so that no one may boast."* When we see passages calling us to perform works and show love while putting our faith into action. Then the works required of us are not for the purpose of elevating one's self to a status above anyone else, or in the end to collect some reward. Moreover, they are a reminder that our continued work for others builds God's Kingdom by showing God's love through these selfless acts.

~ Twelve ~

"Awake, O sleeper, and rise from the dead, and Christ shall give you light." ~ Ephesians 5:14

When speaking of our spiritual morality, officers should consider how we treat other people, what our personal morals are that guide us, how we view the power of our Creator, and how we acknowledge our personal relationship with God through our actions.

The words of Christ bring us back time and again to the simple principal of morality that we as a society, whether of Christian faith or not, should know to be true. In Luke 6:31 Jesus says, *"Do to others as you would have them do to you,"* and in Matthew 7:12, *"So in everything, do to others what you would have them do to you, for this sums up the Law and the Prophets."*

C.S Lewis wrote in *Mere Christianity*, *"Men are mirrors, or "carriers" of Christ to other men. Sometimes unconscious carriers."* And, *"That is why the Church, the whole body of Christians showing Him to one another, is so important."* Understanding that the "Church" is not just a building that we go to on Sundays or a special occasion, helps us to see the collective majority as the "whole body of Christians." This message of *mirroring* each other calls those who declare they are the children of God to action and requires that those actions are not kept at the personal level. We should not leave these responsibilities solely to the physical Church, but instead have a conscious collective of moral duties as the body of Christ.

1 Corinthians 10:24 states, *"Let no one seek his own good, but the good of his neighbor."* Philippians

2:3-4, *"Do nothing from rivalry or conceit, but in humility count others more significant than yourselves. Let each of you look not only to his own interests, but also to the interests of others."* We are warned against self-serving behavior in Proverbs 18:1, *"Whoever isolates himself seeks his own desire; he breaks out against all sound judgment."* And in James 3:16, *"For where jealousy and selfish ambition exist, there will be disorder and every vile practice."*

God wants us to cultivate not only our work but our personal lives with humility, the opposite of which is pride. Do I need to remind you it was through pride that the devil became the devil (Isaiah 14 & Ezekiel 28:12-18)?

Proverbs 16:18 states, *"Pride goes before destruction and a haughty spirit before a fall."* Pride leads to a spiritual end, leaving no room for love and condemning any possible commitment to the spiritual needs of others. Pride cuts off the path to a relationship with God, the very nature of the sin, promoting self-worship. Not to say that praise is immoral but do not place yourself above others for doing something morally right. Your delight should be in the act, not in yourself. We should humbly accept praise, not demand it. A person full of pride only accomplishes tasks to satisfy their needs, whereas service provided through humility fosters love in others, then welcoming praise that is fruitful for the giver and receiver.

Some people would have you believe that the simple thought of wanting to live a selfless life is a selfish action, simply because we are acknowledging ourselves as conscious beings. They say this because they believe in choosing to be selfless we are exercising our own will, when in fact we are alleviating our own will and submitting to the will of God. The truth is when we acknowledge that we are living, breathing creations that can place the needs of others before our own, and do so willingly to the point of ultimate sacrifice, we not only learn the divinity of life but enjoy it as well.

Impossible, some may say, or even a man choosing to surrender to the will of God is a selfish action at heart. People who believe this come to the conclusion that men only praise God out of mortal fear of Him, being the Creator of all things. That assumption in this author's opinion is as foolish as saying that prayer only works due to my belief in it. Does Jesus not intercede for me? Did they not read that nothing is impossible for God? At the heart of the New Testament are the directions for conversion from the selfish lives of walking dead men to a new life in kinship with God, then being His children.

In Luke 9:23-24 Jesus says, *"If anyone would come after Me, he must deny himself and take up his cross daily and follow Me. For whoever wants to save their life will lose it, but whoever loses their life for me will save it."* Jesus also said, *"Very truly I tell you, no one can enter the kingdom of God unless they are born of water and the Spirit. Flesh gives birth to flesh, but the Spirit gives birth to spirit"* (John 3:5-6).

Of course, one could only be selfish in the flesh, but through conversion we are indeed born again in the spirit, and due to this new life can become selfless in Christ. The idea in general would be, *my personal convictions aside*, that even if we couldn't be selfless, shouldn't we at least strive to be? And, if we don't want to be selfless, shouldn't we at least be honest about it? Sometimes people need to be reminded that doing good works for selfish reasons doesn't make you good, it just makes you good at being selfish.

In the interest of God's Kingdom, we not only speak of this new life but show it through our actions holding tight to our convictions. Aside from pointing out the obvious perfect example of selflessness, Christ, I believe most would suggest that it is not possible for any man to again display Christ like selflessness, especially in this day and age while in the course of our duties as police officers. I, on the other hand, would offer you the case of Corporal Desmond Thomas Doss.

Desmond Doss joined the United States Army in April of 1942. Of the 431 uniformed men that received the Congressional Medal of Honor, one was presented to Doss, who during combat did not kill a single enemy soldier. Doss served his country and was willing to risk his life to preserve freedom. Classified a conscientious objector, Doss did not believe he would be required to carry a weapon and intended on serving as an Army combat medic. Doss's convictions were paramount to him. He firmly attested his personal belief that he should not take another person's life. He believed it was his duty to obey God and serve his country, but his refusal to carry a gun led to his persecution as many tried to intimidate him and declared him mentally unfit for the Army.

Desmond served in combat on the islands of Guam, Leyte, and Okinawa. In May 1945, Desmond's division was trying to capture the Maeda Escarpment, a daunting embankment the soldiers called "Hacksaw Ridge". After enemy forces rushed them in a vicious counterattack, officers ordered an immediate retreat. Less than one third of the men were able to descend the ridge to safety. Doss disobeyed orders and ran back into the bombardment of death determined to rescue as many men as he could without a weapon or soldier at his side. His selfless acts on May 5, 1945 resulted in the lives of at least seventy-five men being saved. Doss continued to display selfless service throughout the following assaults. Days later, after being severely wounded in an unsuccessful night raid, Doss insisted that another man be taken first before rescuing him.

In a 2003 interview Doss began talking about a soldier who he had helped while at Hacksaw Ridge. Doss stated that when he found the soldier there was blood covering his face and eyes, stating that he had to use water from his canteen to wash the blood away. Doss said that upon washing the man's face, the soldier's eyes came open and he "just lit up" saying that he thought he had been blind. Doss replied, "If I hadn't got anything more out of the war than that smile he gave me, I would have been well repaid." Wherever could you find a more selfless statement than that?

It was possible for Doss to stand by his convictions, unwavering in his faith, in the midst of bloody war, armed only with his trust in God and his ability to serve, only to feel he would have been overcompensated with a smile. How much easier should it be for us to serve selflessly in our own communities?

Ephesians 2:6-7 tells us, *"God raised us from death to life with Christ Jesus, and he has given us a place beside Christ in heaven. God did this so that in the future world he could show how truly good and kind he is to us because of what Christ Jesus has done,"* adding in verse 10, *"God planned for us to do good things and to live as he has always wanted us to live. That's why he sent Christ to make us what we are."* Christ calls us to life in Him, and it is through this new life that we put the fear of this world to death and allow ourselves to find true freedom, so that we may serve others as Christ did for us.

Another point of interest from the story of Desmond Doss is the fact that although he did not believe in taking another person's life, he did not stand in judgment of his fellow soldiers but instead supported them and risked his life to save theirs. Doss's actions would suggest that he did not care about the beliefs held by others or consider them flawed and unworthy of being saved. Doss was a symbol of faith, gallantly offering his life in service so that others may live. There is no way of telling if his selfless actions brought others to a closer relation with Christ, but I would imagine if it was one out of a thousand, he would still be content.

Does that not echo the teachings of the New Testament? Jesus offered himself so that all lives could be saved, not just the lives of those who agreed with Him or treated Him well. *All* lives. Jesus showed His love for us not only on the Cross but in all His actions leading up to His crucifixion. He didn't say, "wait until the battle is won to share love," but to build His Fathers Kingdom now.

In Matthew 28:18-20 Jesus tells his disciples, *"All authority in heaven and on earth has been given to Me. Go therefore and make disciples of all the nations, baptizing them in the name of the Father and of the Son and of the Holy Spirit, and teaching them to obey everything that I have commanded you. And remember I am with you always, even unto the end of the age."*

We shouldn't consider if someone deserves the message of Christ but remember instead that Jesus died so that the offer of salvation could be presented to every person, believer or not. I recognize that it may seem foreign to offer the word of God to some of the colorful people officers contact. We don't tend to see much change in most offender life styles, no matter how many times we are called to speak with them, investigate them or arrest them. Even if our words were to fall on deaf ears, sometimes the best thing we can do is serve and let our lives reflect the convictions we profess. If we live the moments we are given to guide others to Jesus, the message will be delivered at some point to someone.

~ Thirteen ~

"Even youths shall faint and be weary, and young men shall fall exhausted; but they who wait for the Lord shall renew their strength; they shall mount up with wings like eagles; they shall run and not be weary; they shall walk and not faint."
~ Isaiah 40:30-31

At this point all I can do is hope that God's message has not been lost throughout this small glimpse into one officer's life. There has been a whole lifetime of stories I have left unpenned, but I assure you, you've read nothing but the truth, be it reflections of my life or the words of God.

I was compelled to write this book by God. This was not to supersede anything written in the Bible, but to offer illustrations of God's words in living testimony. I am not saying that in order to be a police officer you must be a Christian, but simply offering the example of a man named Jesus and biblical text as a guide to be a servant in a field that requires service. I attempted to stay away from quoting outside of the Bible because I assumed that most of the people who would want to read this style of book, would probably have the same convictions as me, and found it essential to convey those beliefs.

You have been shown examples of my failures within these pages. I have been far from a perfect example at times in my life and have found myself misled by my own understandings, however, I have a well-founded affirmation of faith. I believe that God is my Creator and heavenly Father. I believe that He sent His only begotten Son, Jesus, into the world as man and that He (Jesus) suffered and died as a sacrifice to atone for our sin. I believe that Jesus rose from the dead and intercedes with His Father for us in Heaven.

Whether or not you believe as I do, the example of Jesus's servitude is exceptional and as presented throughout this work, something I believe necessary if we truly wish to be servants of God. We can still be good officers and accomplish great works, but I believe that if we submit our trust and control to God, accept His forgiveness, and let His word lead our lives, then we can accomplish much greater things, and effect more people with acts of love and kindness. Through Christ-like actions, officers can bring about not only a change in the Force but a change in the people we come into contact with each shift.

The words I have presented will not offer you a life outside of pain, heartache, inconvenience or suffering, or a life outside of this world that is. They may not even offer a complete answer, but they will set you on a path to seek God's grace and find hope in the salvation of a new life. A new life where you seek to let God use the work of your hands to the true betterment of others' spiritual health and give you a new life as a peace officer that will allow your service of the public to be just, fair, and compassionate.

As police officers we are called to set an example in this life. How much more of an example and benefit will we be to others if we follow the tenets set forth by Christ? Even if you personally believed Jesus was only a man, does that make His actions any less praiseworthy? Does He not set a standard that we should all be trying to meet?

Officers know there is enough evil in this world.

We have taken a vow to fight that evil. We have sworn an oath to serve our communities in safe-guarding life and property, protecting the innocent against deception, the weak against oppression or intimidation, and the peaceful against violence or disorder.

In Matthew 9: 35-38 we are reminded that the workers are few. *"Jesus went through all the towns and villages, teaching in their synagogues, proclaiming the good news of the kingdom and healing every disease and sickness. When he saw the crowds, he had compassion on them, because they were harassed and helpless, like sheep without a shepherd. Then he said to his disciples, "The harvest is plentiful but the workers are few. Ask the Lord of the harvest, therefore, to send out workers into his harvest field."*

Truly evaluating ourselves, a lot of us in public service get caught up in being the *"sheep dog"* and forget the vital role of the Good Shepherd. Don't expect your badge to be a symbol of compassion, let your life be evidence of it. Words are just words unless they are put into action, and sheepdogs are just dogs unless the truly care for the sheep. The sheep are not lower than us, and we're not superior to the sheep. We have only decided to take on the responsibility of protecting, in joy, that which is most dear to God.

In Matthew 14:22-33 Jesus's disciples were in fear when they saw Him walking on water, but Jesus immediately said to them, *"Take courage! It is I. Don't be afraid."* Peter replied, *"Lord, if it's you tell me to come to you on the water."* *"Come,"* He said. Then Peter walked on the water and came toward Jesus. But he became afraid and, beginning to sink, cried out, *"Lord, save me!"* Immediately Jesus reached out his hand and caught him. *"You of little faith," he said, "why did you doubt?"*

We try to "walk on water" every day. God challenges us to push our faith beyond boundaries and develop a borderless trust in our Savior Jesus. Just as in scripture, Jesus calls us out to Him, and tells us not to be afraid. Not matter how turbulent your waters are, Jesus is there, offering a way through the sin and shame that bury grace. What will you do when He calls you out of the boat? Stop leaning on your own understanding and put your trust in the one who will keep your head above the water.

So, here is my advice to you, police officer or not. If you don't want drama in your life then don't have it. Trust me, the concept becomes simple when you believe God is in control. God tells us that we won't add one day to our lives by worrying, so if you're able to place your personal problems in a public forum then you should be able to place them at the feet of the Cross. Learn that the same breath you waste to complain about something is the same breath you can use to pray about it, and place God above all things. Pray to be the father or mother God calls you to be. Pray to be the husband or wife God calls you to be, and after that, pray to be the officer God calls you to be.

Don't allow fear to hinder you from doing your job when God calls upon you. John 14:27 says, *"Peace I leave with you; my peace I give you. I do not give to you as the world gives. Do not let your hearts be troubled and do not be afraid."*

I would be lying if I did not say I was full of anxiety while attempting this work. The thought of putting my weaknesses on paper with the potential for anyone to read them really scared me. I wondered if people would judge me or if it would have an effect on my job, but I felt God pulling me toward His message and His desire that I share it. Fear kept me from writing at many times, but I trusted in the Lord and prayed for guidance and strength to deliver His message. I pray no matter what you may think of my shortcomings, you will look past my flaws, and view the hope that I have seen in Christ.

Please work out difficulties with others in a civil manner. People think it is so hard to be human or speak to each other. People don't listen to hear anymore, they listen to speak back with some pre-loaded shot or insult. Our country has created a culture that is always on the defensive. Hear each other out! Listen to each other. A feeling doesn't have to be an argument. People are not always going to feel the same way about things as you do, respect that, just as the other should respect you. You don't have to agree.

Romans 12:18 tells us, *"If possible, so far as it depends on you, live peaceably with all."* And Proverbs 19:11, *"Good sense makes one slow to anger, and it is his glory to overlook an offense."* Remind yourself daily that we are called to love one another as found in John 13:34, *"A new commandment I give to you, that you love one another: just as I have loved you, you also are to love one another."* Go twenty-four hours without being offended by anything... you'll be surprised what you can learn.

Don't let bitterness into your heart. Bitterness will eat up every cell of your being. It will take you over completely and quickly. It is the most devastating thing you can do to yourself, aside from being prideful. Ephesians 4:31 *says, "Let all bitterness and*

*wrath and anger and clamor and slander be put
away from you, along with all malice."*

I know that not grieving properly led to a horrible bitterness inside of me. I learned to grieve things as they come and not let the events of the job weigh down my heart.

Know that you are loved. You are! God loves you. He always has and always will. He loves you so much that he sent his only begotten son to die for you, so that you may have everlasting life. What gift is better than that? Has anyone else made a sacrifice in your life to give you such a chance at redemption? I would lay down my life for all of you, but it wouldn't save your soul.

Know that whatever you do, you have a purpose. Wake up, get out of bed. God has given you this day, so no matter how tough yesterday might have been, get up, get dressed, go out, and take the day on knowing He is walking with you. God gives you each day, don't waste it. I come to work every morning and as soon as I walk in the door, I'm cracking some joke. It's my first attempt to have a positive interaction that I control. I do this no matter what type of night I had, or how my morning has started because it can set the tone for the rest of the day. I also do this to lead by example and show people how they need to come to work, feeling energetic and blessed.

Ephesians 1:11 states, *"All things are done according to God's plan and decision; and God chose us to be his own people in union with Christ because of his own purpose, based on what he had decided from the very beginning."*

Start asking yourself every morning, 'what is Gods purpose for me?' Stop viewing things as obstacles, start viewing them as ways to learn and chances to further God's Kingdom.

If you're wrong, say so. It's okay to be wrong; it's unwise to not admit it. Knowing you are not perfect is good, using it as an excuse is reckless. Remember to forgive others and to receive forgiveness yourself. Grace is a great gift, any day, any season, and so is mercy. Have compassion for all people, not just some of them, and take advantage of the opportunities you are given to display it. Use the words "I love you" every day and mean it. Hugs really do break barriers, so give them often.

I've been through some trials and bad places. I've seen things I never wanted to, and no one should. I've dealt with people on their worst of days and lowest of lows. Every day I get up and put on my vest. It's the one moment I stop and question myself, my one chance to say, 'no more.' I made my wife that deal when I started. That if the day came I couldn't put on my vest, I wouldn't be an officer anymore. I used to think I put that vest on every day because of all the wicked in this world, my chance to do something about it. The bad, the evil, those who take away what we hold dear, and take advantage of others but I was wrong. I may have seen ugly things, and yes, they have affected me, but I realized a long time ago, grief isn't what drove me, and pain was not the reason I put on my vest. It was the good people. The upright, genuine, selflessly caring people that I've seen do extraordinary things, and display genuine acts of kindness. These good contacts fueled me every day. Those people were the ones that helped me put on my vest, and they are still the reason I continue to this day. I urge you to find that good contact and be ardent in your work.

Paul states Romans 8:28, *"And we know that for those who love God all things work together for good, for those who are called according to his purpose."* And *"Do not be slothful in zeal, be fervent in spirit, serve the Lord,"* in Romans 12:11. You must eagerly work to serve God's Kingdom and remember that He will provide through our plight as reminded in Psalm 34:17-20. *"When the righteous cry for help, the Lord hears and delivers them out of all their troubles. The Lord is near to the brokenhearted and saves the crushed in spirit. Many are the afflictions of the righteous, but the Lord delivers him out of them all. He keeps all his bones; not one of them is broken."*

Sacrifice goes beyond just our lives, but I would have given mine my first day and I would still give it now. Know that every single officer who wakes up and turns their back on their world does so because they will not turn their back on you. You're worth it.

So, where do we go from here? On my worst days, when I felt as though there was nothing left to offer, I still cared enough to put on my uniform. The strapping on of my vest and duty belt was an action of faith, a symbol of hope that guided me through my poor condition and beckoned me to see there were still people who needed help, just like me. There was still good work to be done and there still is.

Make no mistake, the ability for me to go to work, even when I felt useless, was never money related. I truly cared for others at a time when I couldn't be bothered to care for my own welfare. People depended on me to be a police officer, and beyond that, God called on me to be a servant. God placed me in circumstances that gave rise to some of my greatest passions, and kept me hanging on to an existence, which at times, felt futile. The Lord guides us through the Spirit even when our faith is at an all-time low, and we can feel that voice calling us back to the mission of furthering God's Kingdom. I was a broken person, a sinner from the very beginning, but God's amazing love provided hope daily through positive encounters and interactions, allowing me to see that a crippled individual like me could still make a difference. The Lord called me to wake up and run to a new life in Him.

There are officers out there who will not agree with my position, people who do not affirm to my beliefs, but if I do not hold fast to my convictions, what good is my integrity as a peace officer? I beg of you, let every moment of your life, in and out of uniform, point to Jesus. Shame awaits every step misplaced, so learn to accept forgiveness, knowing God wants you to rely on His strength. No one understands your needs and can deliver you from affliction better than He can.

When you complete your tour of duty, I challenge you to evaluate your work. Consider if the fruits of your labors bring about a prosperous result for the offenders and victims you contacted. Were your actions a reflection of your faith? If not, then I plead with you, pray to God and ask Him to open your eyes so that you may see a way to further His Kingdom through your position as an officer. Pray that God will give you the courage, strength, and wisdom to fulfill your obligations to the people entrusted in your care. Treat all those you meet as though they are your brother or sister in Christ.

All officers have seen their fair share of lost

causes. I assure you, any time you use your authority to exert God's will that you spread His message, the cause is not lost but indeed supported. The responsibility is not left to us to make others develop a personal relationship with Christ, but the will of God is that we show others that possibility through our actions.

How could anyone exercise their faith, walking into a world that is daily overwhelmed by evil and sin? With Jesus as our hope and God as our strength, we can embrace the battle and make an impact for Christ by conducting ourselves as faithful Christian servants.

Everything we do is owed to the grace of God and our salvation in Christ. Be diligent in your labors and encourage others in our profession. The grace of God implanted in you along with your good abilities and naturally acquired skills are gifts to minister through your works and be good stewards in a wicked and despicable world. So, I leave you with this statement.

What good is our work? What good are the things we've done if only to benefit ourselves? We do such works for a greater good, with a hope above all others, to the end of such a great purpose, and for what? Not the greater good of our souls, but for the good of those souls endeared to us through an oath by our own lips. That light might triumph night and the day wake us in the grace of our Lord.

God bless and stay safe.

~ * ~

Dear Young Officer,

First, let me begin by welcoming you to law enforcement. This career field has a long-standing belief that we truly serve the interest of our communities, and the badge we wear reflects the oath we took. Our communities expect fairness, respect, and that officers will conduct themselves in an intelligent and productive manner. It is indeed them that you work for. We chose that when we became officers, and you chose it when you accepted that commission.

Don't make things personal. You can't overstep the powers entrusted to you. Conduct yourself in a manner that reflects your superiors, that shows intelligence, professionalism, and an eagerness to serve your community. Don't be coarse, abrasive or harsh, but use language reflective of the badge you wear and the oath you spoke. Don't allow personal feelings to compromise your integrity, and refrain from acting out of malice or ill will. Always conduct yourself as though the world is watching.

You will need to understand that law enforcement is the same nationwide, its uniform, but the way we conduct our enforcement and ourselves as professionals varies. Our philosophy is doing the right thing, having strong morals, and above all, having integrity.

You are an extension of your brothers in blue as well as your chief. In turn, you will be viewed as a reflection of them both. Keep this in mind as you serve.

During your tenure you will work in many different aspects of law enforcement. You will see and field an array of calls and crimes. Many of the things you will need to know can't be taught in a small amount of time but will be learned as you progress in your career. A majority of your work in your community is the deterrence of crime. You will need to learn your community and the people in it. You will have to familiarize yourself with its streets and residences. You will have to work hard to be able to serve a community that respects you, because you will have to work harder to give them a community they can respect.

This is a dangerous job. We all know it. You've seen it or read about it. And now, you'll live it. You will get hurt. You may have to fight for your life. You may take a life. You will have to make sure that not only you, but your brothers make it home after every single shift. Listen to your radio and keep up with your fellow officers. Don't make a habit of disregarding your back-up, especially when it comes to your mental health.

Now that the basics are out of the way, let us get down to the meat of it all.

There is nothing of this world that will prepare you for the ride you are about to go on. You are going to see the ugliest of people and more horrid things than I could ever describe. You will become callous. At some point, you may become void of all feeling. You are at risk of reaching darkness you never felt possible. Your heart will hurt in ways you've never known. You will witness murders, suicides, abuse, filth, and unimaginable evil.

There is a huge possibility you will cut yourself off from everyone in your life. You are at risk of divorce, alcoholism, and suicide. You might also reach out for help and not get it. This world is cruel, and if you didn't already know that, you will soon. Most people are sheltered, you will not be. You will have to hold your tongue when others don't. You will have to sacrifice more than what you were ready to. You will have to act strong at your weakest moments. You will have to show relentless bravery when you are scared to death. You will think you are invincible to fear while it surrounds you unknowingly. It will be easier for you to walk up to a vehicle, all alone, in the middle of nowhere with any given list of unknowns, than it will be to talk to your spouse and others about your day.

You will find giving advice is easy but living it yourself is harder.

You will start being more comfortable in your uniform than you are in your own home. When this happens, stop. Do not let work become your safe haven. You have a home for a reason, and that uniform has a department for a reason. If you are always acting with integrity, honor, and discipline, then you will not have to change the person you are at either place. You will only change what you're wearing.

You will work long hours. You will be tired, hungry, and some days you will feel like quitting. You will see brothers fall. Some days you will cry in silence. Sometimes you will feel alone. Often you will feel unloved.

But you are not alone, and you are loved. People care for you. People want your help. People will support you. People will cry when you are hurt. They will stand up with you and say, "no more." You will see that you can make a difference in the face of adversity.

You will find it is okay to say you need help.

The acts you can take legally may be limited, but your ability to act in love never is. You can serve in love and effectively police.
Keep your statutes ready on your mind but keep Gods statutes written on your heart.

There can be justice through peace. You can make a difference every day, and you are the one who chooses what kind of difference that is.
Be a guardian of the people, a warrior on the path to changing hearts.

Everyone is watching you. Everyone will talk about you. People will look up to you or down at you. Take every opportunity to be the hands and feet of Christ. Give no reason for anyone to fault you.

Know when you are wrong. Don't be afraid to admit it. Take every chance to change it.
Your acts will define you. Let your acts be a reflection of love, your badge a symbol of faith, and your uniform an image of service.
You are a public servant, you are a police officer, but most importantly, you are a child of God called upon to offer up grace in the face of failure, peace in a time of chaos, and a love that will triumph over all evil.

Godspeed,

Capt. M.D. Poole

Kudos

"Laced in scripture, this book serves to refocus the hearts and minds of law men and women who serve our communities diligently every single day. Cpt. Poole hit the nail on the head by pointing to our greatest need—Christ, and our most humble act— servanthood".

Kristi Neace, Founder, *Badge of Hope Ministries*; Author of *Under Fire: Marriage Through the Eyes of a Cop's Wife*

"In "Salt & Light" Matt Poole effectively and clearly delivers a message of exhortation and guidance for all who serve. His scriptural guidance and real-life examples will provide you with encouragement and practical steps to becoming the hands and feet of Christ wherever you are."

Adam Davis

Author of *Bulletproof Marriage: a 90-Day Devotional; Behind the Badge: 365 Daily Devotions for Law Enforcement; Spirit & Truth: 52 Devotions for Law Enforcement;* and *On Spiritual Combat: 30 Missions for Victorious Warfare.*

In a powerful narrative, Matt Poole shows us how law enforcement officers can find a balance be-

tween the "warrior" and the "guardian" models of policing, and how God's Word, the Bible, and a loving Christian approach to policing, can empower us and equip us to find the servant spirit that is so desperately needed in our world today.

Lt. Col. Dave Grossman

Author of *On Killing, On Combat and Assassination Generation*

"As a veteran police officer who has walked in the darkness, I can attest that the only way to live out your true calling is through a relationship with Jesus Christ. In Salt and Light, author and fellow veteran police officer M.D. Poole lays out the reason behind the need for Christ as a police officer. Poole does not hold back as he shares intimate details from his own battles. Through scripture, Poole reinforces that true courage comes through the ability to show compassion and lies within the heart of a servant. Poole absolutely inspires while giving us wisdom for our walk—with Christ and on the streets."

Jonathan E. Hickory

Police officer, men's church leader, and author of *Break Every Chain: A Police Officer's Battle with Alcoholism, Depression, and Devastating Loss*; and the *True Story of How God Changed His Life Forever*

Bibliography

https://www.allaboutprayer.org/intercessory-prayer.htm

https://work.chron.com/duties-responsibilities-pastors-12586.html Niel Kokemuller- Hearst newspaper LLC 2018

https://desmonddoss.com/bio/bio-real.php

Law Enforcement Officers and Christianity: Toward a Joint Theology for Law Enforcement- Boston D. Ross, SMU 2016- bross@spartans.ut.edu

The Holy Bible- ESV and NIV

Wikipedia®-The Free Encyclopedia- Https://en.wikipedia.org/wiki/2014_killings_of_NYPD_officers

https://en.wikipedia.org/wiki/Shooting_of_Darren_Goforth

References

The Use and Effectiveness of Community Policing in a Democracy- Bertus, Ferreira-National Institute of Justice. Washington, D.C,, 1996.

Https://www.studylight.org/commentaries/mhm/job.html- Matthew Henry- Full Commentary on Job

Thomas Carlyle-(Heroes and Hero Worship (1840), Lecture V) - On Heroes, Hero-Worship, and The Heroic in History-1841- James Fraser

The Holy Bible- ESV and NIV

Signs Amid the Rubble: The Purposes of God in Human History, Lesslie Newbigin - 2003 by William B. Eerdmans Publishing Company.

C.S. Lewis- Mere Christianity.

Niederhoffer, A. (1967) Behind the shield: Police in urban society. New York: Doubleday & Company.

Wikipedia®-The Free Encyclopedia- https://en.wikipedia.org/wiki/Peelian_principles

Law Enforcement Officers and Christianity: Toward a Joint Theology for Law Enforcement- Boston D. Ross, SMU 2016- bross@spartans.ut.edu

William Shakespeare-Henry V

If you found this book useful to you, please leave a review at Amazon.com or wherever purchase was made. If you know someone this book would be useful to, please pass it on and help spread the Word of God. I also invite you to check out www.dwbpublishing.com.

Dancing With Bear Publishing is a full service, innovative Christian publishing house that strives to publish only the best works that glorify God, and help people in their walk with the Lord.

Connect with Matt:

Email –
mdpoole.author@gmail.com

Facebook -
https://www.facebook.com/authormattpoole

Facebook-
https://www.facebook.com/saltandlightpage

LinkedIn –
www.linkedin.com/in/matt-poole-814a37176/

Twitter –
https://twitter.com/MdpooleA

Salt & Light: Being the Hands and Feet of Christ
(in a cruel and dangerous world)

Captain Matt Poole

www.ingramcontent.com/pod-product-compliance
Lightning Source LLC
Chambersburg PA
CBHW021129020426
42331CB00005B/679